# Rome

Rome

Andrew Leach

# Rome

Polity

First published in 2017 by Polity Press

Polity Press
65 Bridge Street
Cambridge CB2 1UR, UK

Polity Press
350 Main Street
Malden, MA 02148, USA

ISBN-13: 978-0-7456-6974-8
ISBN-13: 978-0-7456-6975-5 (pb)

A catalogue record for this book is available from the British Library.

Library of Congress Cataloging-in-Publication Data

Names: Leach, Andrew, 1976- author.
Title: Rome / Andrew Leach.
Description: Malden, MA : Polity Press, 2016. | Series: Cities in world
history | Includes bibliographical references and index.
Identifiers: LCCN 2016011969| ISBN 9780745669748 (hardcover : alk. paper) |
ISBN 0745669743 (hardcover : alk. paper) | ISBN 9780745669755 (pbk. : alk.
paper) | ISBN 0745669751 (pbk. : alk. paper)
Subjects: LCSH: Rome (Italy)--History.
Classification: LCC DG808. L43 2016 | DDC 945.6/32--dc23 LC record available at
https://lccn.loc.gov/2016011969

Typeset in 11/13 Berkeley by Servis Filmsetting Ltd, Stockport, Cheshire
Printed and bound in the United Kingdom by Clays Ltd, St Ives PLC

The publisher has used its best endeavours to ensure that the URLs for external
websites referred to in this book are correct and active at the time of going to
press. However, the publisher has no responsibility for the websites and can
make no guarantee that a site will remain live or that the content is or will remain
appropriate.

Every effort has been made to trace all copyright holders, but if any have been
inadvertently overlooked the publisher will be pleased to include any necessary
credits in any subsequent reprint or edition.

For further information on Polity, visit our website: politybooks.com

*For Mikayla*

# Contents

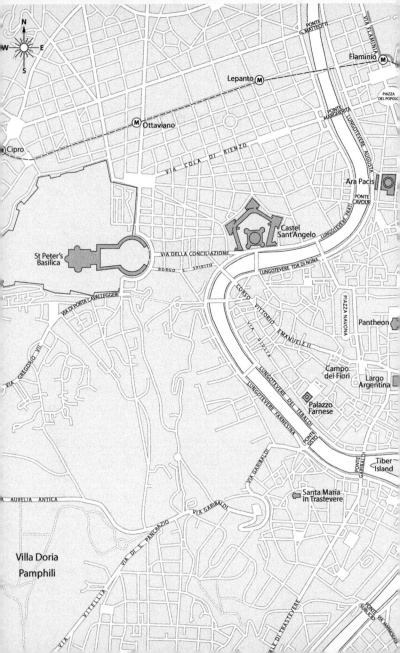

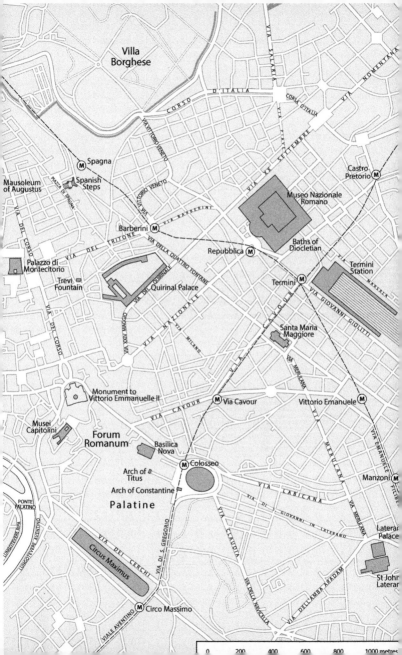

# Preface

A short account of Rome should start in the present – and not because, or not only because, 'the world's history is the world's judgement' (to quote Schiller), but because a book like this really should (and usually does) start with the excuses, caveats and reassurances that will let the author get away with what follows. This book has its limitations, of course, not least being that it has had to set aside much in order to capture in short form the history of a city that extends back nearly three millennia. Rome is the playground of specialists and enthusiasts alike. It is also a scholar's rabbit hole. It deserves every sentence these pages can sustain, but requires the reader to work with the faults he or she finds here – and to build on these pages through his or her own experience, first hand or remote, of Rome as a city in history. In many respects I have written the book I wished I had been able to read on my way to Rome for the first time, and it goes a long way towards giving form to what I have learned since.

In a talk delivered to the American Philosophical Society more than a century ago, Jesse Benedict Carter observed that the 'history of Rome has usually been written with little regard for that material and physical thing, the city of Rome; while the writer on topography is far too apt to see the buildings and the piazzas of ancient Rome as an empty stage, a place for action, but for an action in which he is not professionally interested'.[1] Many scholars have since offered Carter a rebuttal in their work, but the warning remains one worth heeding. I kept this in mind as I worked through a series of encounters with the fabric of Rome, past and present, through which its history unfolds. There are many ways to approach the task at hand. Rome has a history arguably unmatched in richness by any city on the globe. These pages could address economics, population, religion, mythology, water, the family, politics, society, art and culture, and they do so, as much as I have something to offer. I have read as widely and deeply as I have dared and tracked my sources along the way for the reader to pick up where I have had to leave off. But my home base is the history of architecture, and I have used buildings, monuments, city streets and the intentions bound up in them to offer a series of historical sketches that cultivates a view of Rome as a city that shapes and is shaped by history. I have set out to demonstrate what most visitors to Rome will instinctively understand: that the fabric of this ancient city presents moments of mediated contact with the past.

This book presents Rome as a city that demands an encounter with history while being, in itself, resolutely contemporary in each moment, including ours. My goal for what follows is therefore simple in its intent, even if difficult to execute: to offer something of a quick episodic tour of the city's fabric – extant and otherwise, tangible or not – to orientate the reader's own encounter with Rome. These pages negotiate the pregnant gap between this city as a fact in the world – something you can stand on, regard or walk into while trying to take a selfie – and its image as something you can conjure or convey. It is not a guidebook, but I hope it offers something to tourists and travellers. It is a starting point for those who need one, and should function from an armchair as well as it does *in situ*.

The grand tourists of the past needed to pit themselves against the dangers of road and sea to reap Rome's reward. We are more fortunate. It is now possible to get a strong sense of contemporary Rome using the 3D renderings of various mapping programs – Apple Maps has been my weapon of choice – and to enrich it with novels and films to overlay borrowed experience. For some, Rome has to be seen first hand to be believed. For others, it exerts its greatest power upon the imagination. Between Rome's image and its artefacts, though, there is a vast scope for interpretation; and with every path taken, innumerable others are left open. It is one thing to revere Rome's apparent eternity, but reverence must be balanced with a healthy tolerance for its perpetual drive towards the present.

This book relies on a large number of sources and mentions many buildings, individuals, artworks and topographical features. I have restricted facts, figures and personnel to what is necessary to make sense of any given passage in which these appear. The chronology at the end of the book offers a linear account of key events to which many hundreds could be added. The best for which one can hope is that this slender volume will draw readers toward those more patient studies which, with the careful consideration that marks the best histories of art, society, urbanism and culture, can take the reader (and the visitor) into an ever more meaningful encounter with the fine grain of this great city.

\* \* \*

This has not been an easy book to write, and it has taken time. At Polity, Andrea Drugan introduced the prospect of a series dedicated to Cities in World History and indulged my early enthusiasms. Elliott Karstadt picked up where Andrea left off and watched patiently as things crept along, while Pascal Porcheron, Ellen MacDonald-Kramer and India Darsley cheered me across the finish line. My thanks to each of them for their astute advice and sustained forbearance. Justin Dyer's careful editing has been essential. Beyond Polity, so many people have offered their insights and thoughts on this project that I am certain to commit a gross sin of omission by starting to name individuals. I am immensely grateful for the advice I have received from friends, colleagues, reviewers and family, and hold none of them accountable for any failings the reader happens to register in these pages.

Writing this book has been an effort through which to share something about Rome as a city steeped in history that offers a starting point and a companion for its exploration. In this, Ruth and Amelia deserve a special mention as my constant companions in Rome – my experience there has been better for sharing it with them.

# Introduction:
# Thinking about Seeing

*An Overview – A Work of Art of the Highest Order –*
*Trajectories – From Analogy to Experience – Books*
*on Rome*

## *An Overview*

Where to start? Standing to one side of the walls of the
Villa Medici in the gardens of the Villa Borghese, you
can take in the sprawling ancient Campus Martius
and beyond – the entire city, or so it might seem. You
are above Rome, more so than if you had climbed the
hundreds of steps that place you at the base of the
lantern capping the dome of St Peter's Basilica – *and*
you get to keep that extraordinary monument in view.
Looking across the arc from west to south, you can
begin to pick out the forms that step forward into the
vista: the dome of St Peter's (figure 0.1, 1), above all,
but also, to the right, the two churches dedicated to
Santa Maria (2 & 3) that stand on the edge of the
massive Piazza del Popolo; the surprisingly imposing dome of San Carlo on the Corso (4); and, further,
the shallow curve of the Pantheon (5); just below, the
incongruous Victorian spire of All Saints' Anglican
Church (6) on the via del Babuino; and off into the

**Figure 0.1:** Rome from the Pincian hill.

distance, a glimpse of the marzipan Monument to
Vittore Emanuele II (*Il Vittoriano*, 7) – the Sardinian
monarch who became first king of a modern united
Italy. Beneath the line of hills that lies definitively
beyond, and ringed by the highway system of *Il rac-
cordo*, from this spot the city takes shape as a massive
aggregation of marble, plaster and concrete. The monuments through which we identify Rome as Rome –
St Peter's, the Pantheon, the Vittoriano – do not stand
apart from the city in time or space, but merely punc-
tuate its sprawling urban fabric.

### A Work of Art of the Highest Order

This is one of several vantage points from which it is
possible to appreciate parts of Rome as a single, complex entity, even if much lies beyond view, and even
if the twentieth-century city bled well beyond the

Aurelian Wall that now divides the city from its suburbs. At the end of the nineteenth century, before the
sprawl took hold, the Berliner Georg Simmel penned
one of the most profound modern meditations on
Rome as an object of contemplation. He writes of the
'indissoluble impression' it leaves on the mind. As a
collection of stuff amassed over centuries and centuries, in which innumerable cultures interacted with
one another on innumerable terms, it should be an
exercise in chaos. But Rome is indifferent to its past,
just as its many and varied parts are indifferent to the
whole to which they together give rise.

> Here, many generations have produced and built next
> to and above one another, without any care for (and
> indeed without entirely comprehending) what came
> before, surrendering to the needs of the day and to the
> taste and mood of the times. Mere chance has decided

which overall form would result from what has come earlier or later, from what is deteriorating and what is preserved, and from what fits well together or clashes discordantly.[1]

Making sense of Rome is not a matter of peeling back its layers. History piles up here, haphazardly. Its profound beauty, Simmel tells us, lies in the 'wide and yet reconciled distance between the arbitrariness of the parts and the aesthetic sense of the whole'.[2] The roped-off holes of archaeological excavation are commonplace, as are the sights of timeworn buildings wrapped in scaffolding (not yet given over to advertising); monuments are banal, and this failure of the 'exception' in Rome allows history to continue building upon itself, and despite itself, as it has always done. Simmel called it 'a work of art of the highest order', accumulating like the sediment that builds up flood after flood, emperor after emperor, pope after pope, endlessly recalibrating its ground-plane and its meaning to those who would look upon it. Its topography is a product, in part, of its antiquity; neighbouring buildings can sit on entirely different levels. 'What makes the impression of Rome so incomparable', he wrote, 'is that in what separates one age from another, styles, personalities and lives which have left their traces here span further than anywhere else, and nevertheless merge into a unity, a mood, and a sense of belonging unlike anywhere else in the world.' Yet whatever cohesion we find here results not from fine intentions: 'the form in which Rome is built succeeds in transforming its fortuitousness, contrasts and lack of principles . . . into a manifestly tight unity.' A unity reinforced ('effectively, impressively and extensively') by the time separating one element from the next.[3] Rome obliges the present to live with the past, and by doing so to come to terms with it. It is not a city of frozen monuments. It is an experience of history.

It has been centuries since the Quirinal hill marked the north-eastern extremity of Rome proper, but one moment at the base of its southern incline illustrates Simmel's observation. The long and busy path of the nineteenth-century via Nazionale casts an almost direct line from the Baths of Diocletian to Trajan's Market and the Imperial Forums. Pausing about half-way along and looking up the slope towards the Quirinal Palace (or Quirinale), one sees several things at once. The via Milano runs perpendicular to the via Nazionale and disappears into the Traforo Umberto I (figure 0.2, 1) – the tunnel built at the outset of the twentieth century to modernize Rome's traffic circulation, appearing in Vittorio De Sica's 1948 film *Ladri di biciclette* (*The Bicycle Thieves*) as the protagonist Antonio pursues what he imagines to be his stolen wheels. Alongside it one can follow the stairs up the edge of the nineteenth-century Palazzo delle Esposizioni (2) towards the Quirinale (3). At the other end of the block one can do the same, ascending the hill along the via Genova, which brings you to the modest gardens that adjudicate

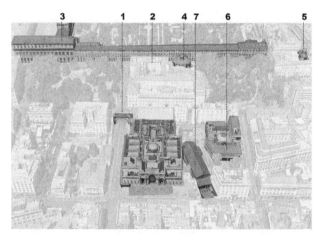

**Figure 0.2:** Prospect view north towards the Quirinale Palace.

between the two fine baroque churches that stand
for the seventeenth-century artistic rivalry between
Gianlorenzo Bernini (Sant'Andrea al Quirinale, 4)
and Francesco Borromini (San Carlo alle Quattro
Fontane, 5). The street corner is marked by a nonde-
script multi-storey building of the kind that blends in
easily with the others along the via Nazionale, in this
case offering cover to a modernist fire station designed
in the 1930s by Ignazio Guidi (6). But between the
display windows of this building and the neoclassical
mass of the Palazzo delle Esposizioni, an old church
extends into the block, at odds with the angles of
its neighbours or the street and dropping, too, down
two metres or so to the fifth-century datum of the
city. Extending sixty metres into this city block, the

modestly gabled roof and arched entrance (narthex) of the fifth-century Basilica of San Vitale belie the extensive alterations to which this church has been subject over its life, reflecting, too, the history of Rome's Christianization. Its presence recalls an earlier stage of the city's history around which tourists obliviously shop, buses and fire engines speed, motorcyclists park, exhibitions come and go and life generally carries on. There is no real sense here that the weight of the past presses terribly much upon the shoulders of the present.

Imagine Simmel coming to terms with this: a city scene being built up in the very decades around the moment in which he was writing. The history of modern cinema has acclimatized us to taking in the incongruity within any given frame of the very old coexisting with the very new in its depictions of Rome. But Simmel's reflections will have come not from the city as represented but from the city as walked, following the paths that the first-time visitor would be remiss in failing to rehearse: a wander through the ancient forums, a hike up to the four fountains from Piazza Barberini, a stroll along the via Appia (Antica), past the monumental fragments of an imperial age and the catacombs marking the ascendancy of the next; the Colosseum, Trevi Fountain, Pantheon, Piazza Navona; St Peter's, the Ponte Sant'Angelo, adorned with the angels of Bernini, and the imposing drum of Hadrian's mausoleum, the Castel Sant'Angelo, on the Tiber's western banks; the baths, the theatres, the circuses, the churches; and beyond the city, the gardens of the Villa d'Este or Hadrian's Villa at Tivoli.

These monuments populated the 'postcards' of tourists both grand and ordinary, and were already, in Simmel's age, the things to see. Even if, today, you were to hire a scooter or hit the cobbles to check them off your list, you would have little change from a long weekend. Yet whether Simmel cast his eyes over Rome from the vantage of the lantern of St Peter's, the steps of Trinità dei Monti, or nearby, like us, from the edge of the Villa Borghese, one can imagine him surveying this city in its dense entirety as he captured the 'image that governs Rome: the immense unity . . . which is not torn apart by vast tension of its elements'.[4]

## Trajectories

In forging a first impression of Rome, film is our friend, and if Simmel offers us a way to stand apart from the city and make sense of what we see, the camera has time and again shown us how we might move *through* it – drawing, as it were, individual paths to populate the impression with detail. One could reconstruct the frenetic route taken by Roberto Benigni's taxi driver in *Night on Earth* (1991) or Nanni Moretti on his summertime *dérives* through Rome's vacated suburbs in *Caro diario* (*Dear Diary*) (1993), or the character Jep Gambardella on his epic nocturnal tours in *La grande bellezza* (*The Great Beauty*) (2013). Few scenes, though, capture Simmel's theme of a unity holding fast in spite of its tensions as well as the first minutes of Federico Fellini's *La dolce vita* (1960). An American Bell 47 helicopter transports a statue of Christ across the city with a second helicopter in pursuit containing the reporter Marcello Rubini and his sidekick Paparazzo. The first shot tracks their arc across the face of the first-century Aqua Claudia, located in the present-day Parco degli Acquedotti – just beyond the Aurelian Wall in the city's south-east. It is an incongruous sight: the modern technology of flight against the backdrop of this ancient piece of hydrological infrastructure, with the pragmatics of getting a parcel from one point to another confounded by the magic invoked by the Messiah sweeping through the air.

The chopper jumps to the suburb of Don Bosco, alongside the epic film studios of Cinecittà, and follows a small crowd running down the Viale dei Salesiani as the camera pans across the street front of what is now a well-established tree-lined avenue, but which at the end of the 1950s was part of Rome's rapidly developing periphery, still very much a city edge under construction. Just before the shot follows the shadow of the lead Bell across a blank wall that is now long built out, a massive dome enters into view, Rome's second largest after St Peter's itself, belonging to the Basilica of San Giovanni Bosco and consecrated a mere nine months before Fellini's film was released – a document of the modern city in its adolescence.

Like Fellini's Messiah, *La dolce vita* arrived in the midst of Rome's rapid post-war expansion, accommodating the needs of a ballooning middle class making the most of Italy's 'economic miracle' and the arrival of thousands upon thousands of migrants from the country's southern reaches moving towards the industrial north and to Rome as the Republic's administrative centre. This moment is captured as the helicopters pass by a hillside housing precinct, an under-construction neo-realist invocation of the 'traditional' pre-industrial village life to which Italian identity remained bound. It is a testament to the difficulty of shrugging off the values that had shaped the generation that went to war in the summer of 1940, and to the widespread uptake of the public housing estates designed and constructed in the 1950s and '60s. Its aspirations, however, lay alongside the young women we now see sunbathing on the rooftop of the modernist housing block typical of those that populated the wealthy new suburbs in the city's freshly developed north – Parioli and its well-heeled neighbours. A fly-way of the newly installed inner-city bypass system is visible to the left of the shot as the first helicopter passes on its way to St Peter's, and as Rubini and Paparazzo pause to circle the sunbathers overhead, their gestured requests for phone numbers unsuccessful, before following their Saviour along the edge of the Tiber towards his final destination, the Piazza di San Pietro at the Vatican. The astute viewer quickly realizes that the Messiah makes nothing so neat as a simple arc across the Eternal City.

## From Analogy to Experience

This diagonal path across the city's topography, monuments and fabric gathers together several of the
Romes these pages will invoke – a city that changes
as forces within and beyond dictate; a city with
edges challenged by the future taking shape beyond
its limits and by its ever-shifting significance to the
wider world. It is at once a centre and centreless.
Simmel suggests that Rome can only be one thing by
being many things at once. Another giant of modern
thought suggests another way of seeing things. For
Sigmund Freud, the experience of Rome was like an
encounter with memory, its history a kind of burden
sitting on the shoulders of the present.

Even before he first passed through its gates, Rome
loomed large for Freud as an analogy for the workings
of the mind. In *The Interpretation of Dreams* (1899) he
records four occasions on which the city had come to
him while he slept: a dream containing a view of the
Tiber and the Ponte Sant'Angelo, in which he imagined
himself departing from Rome in a train just as he realized that he 'had not so much as set foot in the city' but
divined the view from an engraving; another in which
Rome appeared 'half-shrouded in mist', viewed from
such a distance that he was surprised by its clarity; a
Rome in which the city's 'urban character' had been
given entirely over to wild nature, obliging him to ask
a passing acquaintance for directions; and a fourth in
which he reached an intersection only to be surprised

by the number of placards in his native German.[5] The interpretation of dreams is a job for professionals, but, read simplistically, these vignettes offer an insight into the experience of Rome itself: known only ever in part by its visitors, who must reconcile image with experience, beholden to a false sense of clarity and confronted by the impossibility of an authentic, unadulterated encounter with this city.

Three decades after writing *The Interpretation of Dreams*, Freud invited readers of *Civilization and Its Discontents* (1930) to consider the various forms taken by the city over the course of its history: the Palatine *Roma quadrata*, the city arranged around its seven ancient hills, the city enclosed by the Servian and then Aurelian walls, and so on. He wonders about the traces 'of these early stages [that] can still be found by a modern visitor to Rome'. Some things remain in plain sight: beyond a few gaps, the Aurelian Wall was more intact in 1930 than it is today; fragments of the pre-republican circuit wall (or walls) have been recovered by archaeologists. The visitor with 'the best historical and topographical knowledge' can both 'trace the whole course of this wall and enter the outlines of *Roma quadrata* in a modern city plan'. Yet where the city gives up its earlier forms, its contents have largely been either lost to time or decisively modified and modernized over the centuries. The modern visitor might have the means to locate the sites of specific temples, theatres and palaces, but their structures, suggests Freud, are largely the domain of the past rather than the present, 'occupied by ruins – not of the original buildings, but of various buildings that replaced them after they burnt down or were destroyed'.[6] Freud may have had in mind the large sheets of the *Ichnographia Campus Martius*, drawn by the Venetian architect Piranesi in the middle of the eighteenth century. Certainly, his observations could not resonate more with Piranesi's capacity to invoke an ancient city by documenting what he could find, extrapolating part of the balance on the back of ruins and fragments, and filling in the rest with informed invention.

Freud asks his reader to imagine Rome as a city 'in which nothing that ever took shape has passed away, and in which all phases of development exist beside the most recent'. Consider what we would see: 'the imperial palaces and the Septizonium of Septimius Severus' reaching their original full height on the Palatine hill; the statuary adorning the Castel Sant'Angelo in the medieval centuries in full view; the Temple of Jupiter Capitolinus, where stands the Palazzo Caffarelli on the Capitoline hill; Nero's Domus Aurea along the site of the Colosseum; and the medieval church of Santa Maria sopra Minerva – housing among its artworks Michelangelo's *Christ the Redeemer* and among its sarcophagi that of Renaissance painter Fra Angelico – all in view together with the ancient temple upon which it was built and for which it is named. We would return, too, to the Pantheon (figure 0.3). By standing alongside Bernini's seventeenth-century sculpture of

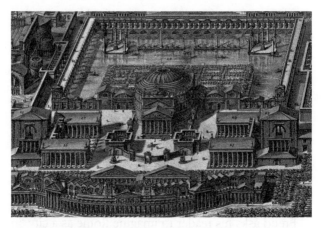

**Figure 0.3:** Giovanni Battista Piranesi, Elevation of the Pantheon and of other Buildings in Its Vicinity, engraving, *Il Campo Marzio dell'Antica Roma* (1762).

the elephant and obelisk on the Piazza della Minerva, one can regard the vast concrete drum of a structure originally raised during the reign of Augustus in the first century AD under the great imperial builder Marcus Agrippa – son of Lucius and thrice consul, the commanding frieze tells us (see pp. 95–103) – and reconstructed twice under the authority of Domitian and Hadrian in turn. Freud imagines a trick of the eye allowing the onlooker to see each phase in the life of these monuments at once. This, he says, is akin to the workings of the mental life.[7]

Freud found in Rome a demonstration of how memories press through into everyday life – and of how these memories can be weighty even as they shape an individual subconsciously. The analogy works just as well for a Rome reconciled to its past: a city steeped in its own history, in which contemporary life demands that one quite literally navigates around those holes in the ground in which the present is processing that which happened long ago. Rome's antiquities break into the present persistently and without pattern. The relentlessness with which the present carries on around them regardless lent Freud an ideal analogy for explaining how we deal with memory. He helps us, too, understand something of how the past, here, is palpable in its presence.

An artwork by Elisabetta Benassi in the permanent collection of MAXXI (the National Museum of the 21st-Century Arts, in Flaminio) offers another take on this. Called *Alfa Romeo GT Veloce 1975–2007*, it consists of an empty car – make and model as advertised – sitting (when properly installed) in a darkened space. Borrowed light picks out the car's general form, a latent menace, before the headlights spring into life, full beam, as a kind of shock. The car is the same model as that driven by the writer and filmmaker Pier Paolo Pasolini on the night of his assassination, 2 November 1975, and Benassi confronts the spectator with this episode in Italy's relatively recent cultural history as one not yet assimilated into an easy narrative – as something that once happened, but in a past beyond that which serves as the immediate backdrop to the present. Pasolini's death is shrouded in secrets that run deep to the heart of Italy's troubled *anni di piombo* – the Years of Lead, shockingly punctuated by the assassination of Aldo Moro in 1978 by the Brigate Rosse, or Red Brigades – in which elements of the radicalized left and right were in open conflict and in which the balance of power between governments at all levels, the Church, political groups and organized crime regularly gave way to acts of violence and disruption. Benassi's centrepiece – the car – recalls all that one might prefer not to know in Rome's more recent history.

We began with Simmel's reflections on Rome, but Benassi brings to mind a line from another of his three portraits of Italian cities. Simmel writes of Venice (arguably Rome's counterpoint) as 'dreamlike', a stage over which actors pass without in any way changing it. In a setting like this, 'reality always startles us'.[8] Rome, by contrast, is a city of realities that startle, shattering the illusion of 'eternity' and the narratives that it demands to reveal something that expands and contracts, rises and falls, impresses and disgusts. Even Simmel insisted that we can only ever take Rome in as a whole to sense its beauty as a thing entire. We cannot pause before too much *in particular*.

### Books on Rome

To Simmel, Fellini, Benassi and Freud, we could add many other voices contemplating this city and that for which it stands, all trying to make sense of its complexities and contradictions. One more deserves note before we move on. In a recent reflection on 'why ancient Rome matters to the modern world',[9] classical historian Mary Beard observed: 'The truth is that Roman history offers very few direct lessons for us, and no simple list of dos and don'ts.' But the folly of ignoring this truth has been repeated across the centuries. The symbols and imagery of the ancient city – the city at the height of its reach (and decadence) – have regularly returned in moments where geo-political ambition and ideological security have reinforced one another. Beard writes of the temptation to view the contemporary plight of western society against the seemingly eternal measure that Rome offers. As much as Rome occupies the individual imagination, fed by paintings, comics, films, novels, etchings and history classes, it has also and often served as a yardstick for those imperial projects that found their measure in the empire founded by Augustus. The middle of the twentieth century witnessed such an invocation – the idea of Rome's glorious imperial history and unassailable values underwriting Italy's misguided imperial aspirations in the decades preceding the Second World War.

Against this backdrop, one writer made a gesture that should seem profound to anyone who reads and writes history. In October 1931, the 29-year-old poet and aviator Lauro de Bosis, an antifascist pamphleteer, took to the skies above the Italian capital to distribute two documents to its citizens. The first exhorted the King of Italy, then Vittorio Emanuele III, to act in a way that was worthy of his office and to curb the power of Mussolini and the spread of his fascist rule. The other was addressed to the citizens of Rome, extolling the virtues of a personal freedom that they had given up all too freely. De Bosis traded fuel load for paper and after a half-hour flight across Rome he drifted out to sea, where he is presumed to have crashed. An extraordinary episode on its own, it takes on greater meaning when read alongside the note he wrote in the early hours of the morning of his final flight and sent to his friend Francesco Luigi Ferrari to publish in the Belgian review *Le Soir*. In a powerful plea to his posthumous readers, de Bosis wrote: 'Besides my letters, I am going to throw out several copies of a magnificent book by Bolton King: *Fascismo in Italia*. As one throws bread on a starving village one must throw history books on Rome.'[10]

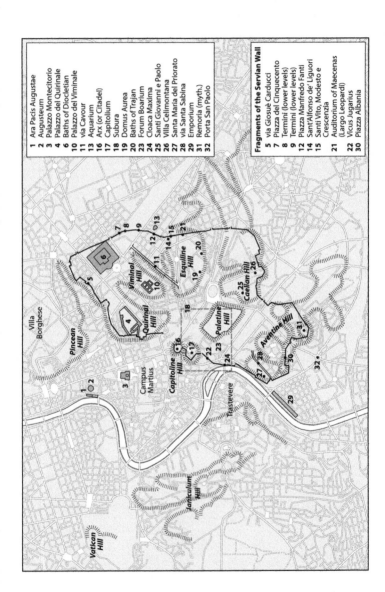

1 Ara Pacis Augustae
2 Augusteum
3 Palazzo Montecitorio
4 Palazzo del Quirinale
6 Baths of Diocletian
10 Palazzo del Viminale
11 via Cavour
13 Aquarium
16 Arx (or Citadel)
17 Capitolium
18 Subura
19 Domus Aurea
20 Baths of Trajan
23 Forum Boarium
24 Cloaca Maxima
25 Santi Giovanni e Paolo
26 Villa Celimontana
27 Santa Maria del Priorato
28 via Santa Sabina
29 Emporium
31 Remoria (myth.)
32 Porta San Paolo

**Fragments of the Servian Wall**

5 via Giosuè Carducci
7 Piazza del Cinquecento
8 Termini (lower levels)
9 Termini (lower levels)
12 Piazza Manfredo Fanti
14 Sant'Alfonso de' Liguori
15 Santi Vito, Modesto e
Crescenzia
21 Auditorium of Maecenas
(Largo Leopardi)
22 Vicus Jugarius
30 Piazza Albania

**1**

# A Matter of Foundations

*At the Ara Pacis Augustae – Romulus and Remus –*
*Aeneas and the Origins of the Romans – Foundations –*
*Archaic Rome – The Servian Wall – A City of Seven Hills*
*– The Forum Romanum – From Settlement to City*

### At the Ara Pacis Augustae

In his biography of the first Roman emperor, the historian Suetonius had Augustus famously observe that he had 'found Rome a city of bricks and left it a city of marble': 'Marmoream se relinquere, quam latericiam accepisset.' The year 2014 marked two millennia since the emperor and his marble city finally parted company – the former to enter the afterlife, the latter to continue bearing witness to the passage of time – and the biographer captures perfectly the absolute transformation to which Augustan Rome bore witness. Once the centre of its own world, one settlement among several, it had become the centre of *the* world.

To mark his achievements in perpetuity, Augustus conceived of three monuments: a domed, circular mausoleum (main map, 2), now called the Augusteum, that would house his funeral pyre (ustrinum) and a dynastic tomb; a massive sundial, the Solarium Augusti,

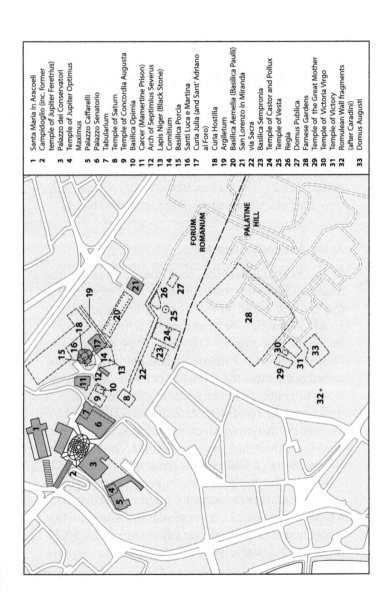

1 Santa Maria in Aracoeli
2 Campidoglio (inc. former temple of Jupiter Feretrius)
3 Palazzo dei Conservatori
4 Temple of Jupiter Optimus Maximus
5 Palazzo Caffarelli
6 Palazzo Senatorio
7 Tabularium
8 Temple of Saturn
9 Temple of Concordia Augusta
10 Basilica Opimia
11 Carcer (Mamertine Prison)
12 Arch of Septimius Severus
13 Lapis Niger (Black Stone)
14 Comitium
15 Basilica Porcia
16 Santi Luca e Martina
17 Curia Julia (and Sant' Adriano al Foro)
18 Curia Hostilia
19 Argiletum
20 Basilica Aemelia (Basilica Paulli)
21 San Lorenzo in Miranda
22 via Sacra
23 Basilica Sempronia
24 Temple of Castor and Pollux
25 Temple of Vesta
26 Regia
27 Domus Publica
28 Farnese Gardens
29 Temple of the Great Mother
30 Temple of Victoria Virgo
31 Temple of Victory
32 Romulean Wall fragments (after Caradini)
33 Domus Augusti

FORUM ROMANUM

PALATINE HILL

casting its shadow across the Campus Martius; and a monument to the 'Augustan Peace', the Ara Pacis Augustae (main, 1), which the sundial would over-shadow each year on 23 September, the autumnal equinox and the emperor's birthday. Each monument entered a state of ruin within the lifetime of the empire Augustus had founded, only to be recovered in piecemeal fashion as the Campus Martius, or Campo Marzio, became increasingly populated with palaces and churches in the early modern era.

Fragments of the Solarium were found from the fifteenth century onwards and placed in their current location before the seventeenth-century Palazzo Montecitorio – once home to the Curia Apostolica and, since Unification, accommodating the Italian House of Representatives (main, 3). Pieces of the Ara Pacis (or what have long been assumed to be such) were also collated from the sixteenth century onwards to form the monument that now sits opposite the forlorn Augusteum, which was restored as part of an urban renewal project conceived under Mussolini's authority in the 1930s. The bimillennial of Augustus' death was a dull affair marked by missed deadlines. The 1937 celebration of his birth, however, was vividly coloured by the cult of *romanità* as ideologues and tastemakers sought to recast Rome as the heart of a new Italian Empire, a natural heir to its ancient imperial forebear. That year saw the inauguration of building works intended to ensure that the Ara Pacis was preserved as a privileged moment within the fascist city – works that were interrupted by war and never resumed. More than half a century later, though, the Ara Pacis found itself encased in a contentious new building designed by the American architect Richard Meier, opening to markedly mixed reviews in 2006.

The significance placed by Mussolini on imperial Rome was hardly the first time that a glorious past had been used to validate present-day claims of authority. Augustus himself built confidently on the bedrock of Rome's myths – two of which, rendered in marble, we meet upon entering Meier's stage (figure 1.1). Only with difficulty can we extract the events depicted on

**Figure 1.1:** Ara Pacis, building by Richard Meier (completed 2006).

the Lupercal and Aeneas panels from the very idea of Rome, and so each deserves our attention.

## Romulus and Remus

Romulus and Remus are everywhere in this city: twin infants sustained by a she-wolf, one of whom would go on to found Rome itself. The medieval, bronze Capitoline Wolf – with its sixteenth-century addition of the twins – has come to stand for Rome as surely as the Eiffel Tower stands for Paris and the Statue of Liberty for New York. (The eighteenth-century art historian Johann Joachim Winckelmann suggested that the wolf was Etruscan, possibly made by the same sculptor, Vulcan of Veii, who carved the reliefs on the Temple of Jupiter Capitolinus. Carbon dating has put it instead as being made between the mid-eleventh and mid-twelfth centuries.) In modern times it was used as the symbol of the 1960 Olympic Games and even now appears on the crest of Rome's premier football team – on almost anything, really, that can be sold at a souvenir stand or market stall. T-shirts, key rings, beanies, barbeque aprons: Romulus, Remus and the wolf, alone in their cave, embody Rome. In the Ara Pacis their story is invoked on the left of the two panels (the Lupercal Relief), which shows the brothers drinking from the wolf in the shade of a fig tree under the protective gaze of their father, depicted as Mars, and the shepherd Faustulus, who found them at the base of the Palatine and raised them with his wife, Acca Larentia.

Standing before the Lupercal Relief is one way to reflect upon this foundation myth. Another is to make the short trek from the Ara Pacis to the Palatine hill (entry through the Forum for a fee) and to the Domus Augusti (House of Augustus: inset map, 33) thereupon, now protected by an incongruous hip roof (and partly visible from the Circus Maximus, or Circo Massimo, that runs along the base of the hill). In 2007, archaeologists announced their discovery of a decorated first-century BC circular chamber beneath the Domus – an apparent celebration of what they claimed to be the very cave in which the twins were said to be raised. It appeared to add substance to the story. Enthusiasm quickly gave way to debate, though, as to the precise identity and patronage of what had first been named the Lupercal, but it is difficult to shake the idea of the emperor literally building his own house upon the embellished grotto in which the idea of Rome was first made possible.

The events held to have followed the discovery of Romulus and Remus on the banks of the Tiber (the course of which having changed over time) comprise what must arguably be one of the best-known stories of antiquity. As is common with siblings, the boys were close, but were also prone to fight, and as they grew into men their conflicts became more pronounced. They were children of the god of war and grandchildren of the king of the principal Latin city of Alba Longa; rulership was in their blood. (Castel Gandolfo, the pope's summer residence, now occupies the site of Alba Longa.) Before the boys had been born, Amulius had conspired to remove his brother Numitor from the throne, kill his male heir and commit his niece Rhea Silvia to life as a Vestal Virgin. Discovering that she had become pregnant (to the god Mars, she claimed) and given birth to twin boys, Amulius instructed that the boys be killed and their mother imprisoned. The boys, as we know, survived. As youths, they worked the slopes of the Palatine hill and tended livestock, playing Robin Hood in their spare time by depriving thieves of their spoils and distributing the takings among the shepherds. An act of retribution saw Remus in the custody of his grandfather, who (like Faustulus at the same time) did his sums and understood the young man to be his grandson. Romulus and his shepherd brethren met Remus at an agreed-upon time and they together overthrew Amulius, King of Alba Longa.

Not content with waiting to inherit Alba Longa from their grandfather, Remus and Romulus instead embraced the prospect of founding a new city (or two new cities, depending on the account) on the very slopes where they had tended flocks with their adoptive father. Romulus built a wall (or dug a trench) to define the extent of a settlement over which he would rule as king. Remus may or may not have founded his own city of Remoria (main, 31) on the neighbouring Aventine hill, but he insulted Romulus' fortifications and showed their weakness by climbing (or jumping) over them, at which point either Romulus or his agent Celer (from whom we have Celeres, royal bodyguards) clocked him fatally on the head with a shovel (or a hoe, or some other deadly implement), thereby clearing up the question of sovereignty and defining for the city its first ruler, after whom, naturally, Rome took its name.

This is the most resilient version of events, recorded three centuries after the fact by Quintus Fabius Pictor. Fabius wrote towards the end of the third century BC, in the years of the Second Punic Wars, when Rome had begun to assert itself as a Mediterranean force and acquire colonies. He helped to make sense of the city's rise and shaped the image that projected its power and authority within the region. The history written by Fabius is now lost to time, but shaped those later histories written by the likes of Polybius, Dionysius of Halicarnassus and Titus Livius Patavinus, known as Livy. Written in the time of Augustus, Livy's history was called *Ab urbe condita* ('from the founding of the city'), borrowing from Fabius to explain the events spanning from Rome's origins to his present day. As such, his rehearsal of the so-called Fabian myth offers a reassuring version of Rome's foundations as a city at a time when, under Augustus, Rome was bedding down fresh footings upon them.

Livy has Romulus disappear at the end of his life, being swallowed up by a storm after offering a sacrifice on the Quirinal hill: perhaps an early instance of senatorial regicide, but with the effect of deifying the founder for subsequent generations. Variations on Fabius (and

Livy after him) abound, and the now-conventional depiction of the twins, wolf, shepherd and wife is one version of a story told every which way. Some writers accord Acca Larentia with either more base or more divine standing, depending on the storyteller; some conflate her with the wolf. Others have Remus survive Romulus, which would put paid to the Fabian punchline. The importance of the story is not, though, simply in identifying a moment in which Rome comes to be: a makeshift weapon finding its mark and a furrow hitting the earth, first gestures defining the city that would rule the world. It rests rather in the potential authority offered by history to the great families of the third and second centuries BC, whose origins, too, one way or another trace back to the Lupercal. It also lies in the promise of Rome's enduring power, secured by the bloodlines and blessings of the gods.

## Aeneas and the Origins of the Romans

Opposite the Lupercal panel in the Ara Pacis is a relief depicting Aeneas arriving at Latium. After the famous ingenuity of the Achaeans saw the Trojans lose their city, the poet Virgil has Aeneas (son of Venus) embark upon an odyssey directed step by step towards the mouth of the River Tiber and the fertile lands occupied by the Etruscans, Sabines and Latins. In the same way as Livy's *Ab urbe condita* (published just a few years earlier) places Romulus and Remus squarely at the birth of the city, Virgil's *Aeneid* adds the wanderings and travails of the hero of Troy to the edifice of Augustan authority as Aeneas makes his way towards 'the destin'd town' (as John Dryden put it), that others might advance, thereafter, towards 'the long glories of majestic Rome'.[1]

Over the centuries, the arrival of Aeneas and the subsequent conquest of the cities of Latium became embedded in the story of Rome's foundation. Augustan-era genealogies offer compelling credentials for Romulus and Remus deep in the Greek bedrock of Mediterranean mythology. Aeneas entered the royal line of Latium through marriage to Lavinia, daughter of the king Latinus, for whom the region is named, and who precedes the twins by fifteen generations. In recounting the foundations of a city that would come to rule the world, Rome's first-century BC historians made its origins resonate with the project of empire and with its (likewise destin'd) renovation under Augustus – purchased with the riches it held to be rightly Roman.

Aeneas' wanderings at Virgil's behest puts deep history in play with the recent past. Destiny may have secured the marriage between Aeneas and Lavinia (who had, before his arrival, been betrothed to Turnus of the Rutuli), but it severed his earlier marriage to the Phoenician queen Dido of Carthage, whom he abandoned to continue his quest. (The chronology does not add up, but in matters such as these the reader needs to be tolerant.) Betrothal and dissolution both resulted in war: in Latium, leading to victory for Aeneas and the rise of his line; and, many centuries later, in the Punic Wars of the third and second centuries BC, where the sustained clash of the Roman Republic with Carthage (waged concurrently with the Macedonian Wars to the east) largely completed Rome's ascendancy over the Mediterranean basin, securing its first colonies beyond Italy and, with them, the real prospect of an empire.

In the first instance, and through the intercession of Latinus, the Trojan refugees were peaceable in their settlement of Latium. Aeneas, though, saw it as the rightful inheritance of his dispossessed people, conducting a sustained and bloody warfare to place the people of Latium under his dominion. Eventually achieving a regional peace, he founded his own city of Lavinium (named for his wife, on the site of the coastal town of Pratica di Mare), which became the principal city of the Latin League. (By the time of Romulus and Remus, that position was held by Alba Longa.) Over time, Aeneas was adopted as the original Roman hero, embodying those qualities celebrated by Rome's governing class in the era of its republic, and eventually by the emperor above all. According to Livy, Venus asked Jupiter (others have her ask the river god Numicus) to make her son immortal, which he did, in the form of the minor deity Jupiter Indiges. After an encounter between the Trojans and the local Rutuli at the Numicus river, his body was never found, which may have been immortalization at work or the consequence of a simple accident. The exploits of Aeneas were nonetheless told and retold over the following centuries, and by at least the fourth century BC had been distilled into a story that, through the Lavinian line, with a mix of Trojan blood, and Latin royalty and divinity, made Aeneas the ancestor of Romulus and Remus and a giant, therefore, of Rome's prehistory.

In the Ara Pacis, the Aeneas panel captures the moment when the Virgilian hero makes landfall at the mouth of the Tiber – a first step bridging one long journey and another. An ill-fated sacrificial sow stands with the two household gods who accompanied Aeneas from Troy: the Penates, to whom Aeneas offers a drink. To his left is a figure who might just be Ascanius Iulius, Aeneas' son and figurehead of the Julian line that ulti- mately gave rise to Gaius Julius Caesar and his adopted son Gaius Octavius, or Augustus, whose likeness else- where on the Ara Pacis monument bears a striking similarity to that of Aeneas. In the *Iliad*, Homer called Aeneas the 'king of man'. Augustus, too, would share this claim and accept its inevitability as a matter deter- mined by the gods. We, though, tend to read the early histories of Rome as a more fragile affair. 'It should never be forgotten,' writes classicist T. P. Wiseman, 'that our picture of the Romans is almost wholly con- ceived from the work of authors writing … at the time when Rome was an imperial power which had defined Rome as different from, and superior to, the peoples it had subjected.'[2] Fragile or not, this picture invites our reflection on the power of a Roman past capable of being insistently present.

## Foundations

It may be premature to speak of Rome's earliest beginnings as urbanization, or of those beginnings as a city, but bound up in the events depicted on the two above-mentioned panels of the Ara Pacis is a play between facts and myth that can be grounded, to an extent, by spending more time on the slopes of the Palatine hill and, at its northern base, in the Forum Romanum – even if all that dates to this time is either lost or buried. The term 'Roma quadrata' describes the roughly square shape of Rome's earliest form as what many think was once a defined and defended hillside settlement on the Palatine. As Rome grew, it absorbed through treaty or conquest other nearby settlements, including those on the Quirinal hill (a traditional site of Sabine settlements) and in Trastevere (an Etruscan town), which would each rightly claim alternative origin stories for Rome based on an arguably older occupation of parts of the contemporary city. As the intersection, though, of a city fabric and an idea, Rome *as Rome* begins on the Palatine.

In the first decades of this settlement, the present-day Forum was a marshy valley between this hill and what might have been the Velian hill (or Velial ridge) – a rise depicted in ancient accounts, but which has long since been levelled. Those who stand behind the idea of an original Roma quadrata call the wall that defined it either the Palatine or, after its supposed author, Romulean Wall. Tradition dates this wall and the consequent founding of Rome to 753 BC, but even in the eighth century the Palatine was no *terra nullius*. Throughout Central Italy, a region of great antiquity, there is considerable evidence of Bronze Age settlement, and on the Palatine itself the oldest structure appears to date to the ninth century BC: a large oval hut on the western slope of the hill (roughly oriented towards the Forum Boarium (main, 23), near to the purported site of the republican-era Temple of Victory (inset, 31), Temple of the Great Mother (Magna Mater) (inset, 29) and Temple of Victoria Virgo (inset, 30), all originally dating to around the end of the fourth century BC. There is more evidence of this structure – posts for wall supports, a general sense of its scale – than of the purportedly more enduring buildings that replaced it around the time of the twins' victory over Amulius. A 'fossa' grave – typically a stone-lined trench – indicates that people lived and died on the Palatine at least as early as the first part of the eighth century BC. Indeed, archaeologists Anna De Santis and Gianfranco Mieli in 2008 reported the discovery of six tombs dating to the eleventh and tenth centuries BC on the site on the north-eastern edge of the Forum Romanum developed in the 40s BC as the Forum Julii or Forum of Caesar. On the two crests of the neighbouring Capitoline hill, the Arx (or Citadel: main, 16) and Capitolium (main, 17), are sites of worship from around the third quarter of the eighth century, likely originating with a temple in honour of the god Jupiter Feretrius that arguably dates to the time of Romulus. The area between these two crests was, according to tradition, a sanctuary for foreigners and called Asylum. It, too, was inhabited from the ninth century BC.

Early Romans, it seems, worked the land and worshipped according to its needs. On the Palatine, there was somewhere to live and somewhere to bury, and on the Capitoline, there was somewhere to make offerings. At the end of the sixth century BC, the Temple of Jupiter Optimus Maximus (Jupiter Capitolinus: inset, 4) joined the Romulean temple of Jupiter Feretrius (inset, 2) on the Capitolium, and was consecrated, in fact, in the first year of the Republic, 509 BC, despite having been vowed by the first of the Tarquin kings after the defeat of the Sabines more than two centuries earlier. (The Palazzo dei Conservatori [inset, 3] and the Palazzo Caffarelli [inset, 5], flanking Michelangelo's sixteenth-century Campidoglio [inset, 4], now overwrite its footprint.) The idea of Rome might not yet have been born before the eighth-century BC adventures of Romulus, but in the artefacts left behind by the people of this time, evidencing their need for shelter, sustenance, death and worship, the city has its most tangible foundations.

The position of archaic Rome among the cities of Latium was initially secured by battle. Romulus was held to have successfully waged war with the powerful nearby city of Veii, as did Servius two centuries later. As Rome was a settlement established on the basis of a victory by shepherds over the king of Alba Longa, its population was founded on a colony of single men of the land and the region's disaffected and dispossessed. The violent abduction of the Sabine women was an early act of deceit that secured wives and children for the first generation of Rome's menfolk, which in turn gave Rome a union of sorts between a new city filled with landless unmarried men and the Sabine people, who were established on the Quirinal hill as well as throughout modern-day Lazio, Umbria and Abruzzo (Sabinium). As the story goes, the new Romans invited their neighbours to a games event intended to impress and befriend, but at a pre-arranged moment the Romans 'fell upon' the daughters of their guests (as Pierre Grimal euphemistically puts it), and kept them as wives.[3]

Tradition has it that this abduction took place around 750 BC, soon after the city's foundation and long before its clear ascendancy above the region's established cities – some of which, like Veii, it would conquer, while absorbing others as it entered into the Latin League and the mutual protections assured to its thirty or so constituent cities. There is as much evidence of this abduction as there is of Romulus' own fratricide, but it has served tradition well by ensuring that the population of Rome would survive beyond its purely masculine founding generation. History accords honour to the Sabine women and those women of other tribes stripped of their daughters that same day for selflessly acting to prevent retribution against those who were now their own husbands.

By the end of the eighth century, there is evidence of enough urban activity to support the image of a structured and organized society at the base of the Palatine and Capitoline hills. For hundreds of years, the Comitium (inset, 14) – a platform for public debate – was at the centre of Rome's civic life. All aspects of that life took place on the adjacent Forum Romanum, which by the start of the sixth century BC was an established setting for worship, trade, rulership, litigation and recreation. Over the course of two centuries, the bases of Rome's urban infrastructure – markets and temples, roads and defences – were for the main part in place. Its people had evolved a considered and popular mode of government corresponding to a complex and functional religious culture. Together they supported the significant change to which Rome was subject over the course of the sixth century: it started out that century as a city ruled by kings and ended it as a republic.

## Archaic Rome

Historians call Rome of the two or three centuries preceding the Republic 'archaic' Rome, a term which spans from the city's murky beginnings to the end of the sixth century and the reconfiguration, therefore, of the social and hierarchical structures under which it had found its feet and flourished. Archaic Rome was ruled by a succession of kings who were, with two important exceptions, elected to their thrones by a curiate assembly. This assembly was comprised of citizens and arranged according to family groups. Up to the reign of Servius Tullius (who ruled 578–535 BC), there were thirty *curiae*, comprised of ten representatives of each of the three familial tribes that tradition dates to the reign of Romulus: the Ramnenses, the Titienses and the Luceres (the origins of which are as opaque as much of the history of this era). Each of these *curiae* was led by a *curio maximus*, who was a mature patrician – one of the nobles descending from the century of men appointed as senators by Romulus. Citizens who were not members of this nobility were called plebeians. The fifth king increased the number of senators to 200, which was further increased to 300 by two of the founders and the first consuls of the Roman Republic, Lucius Junius Brutus and Publius Valerius Publicola. Senators had wide-ranging powers that varied over time, details of which vary, too, from historian to historian. The Senate may or may not have elected the king (who lived in the Regia: inset, 26), or (later) maintained control when a dictator was appointed to address emergencies of various kinds.[4]

During both its regal and republican phases, the Senate (or Curia) met in the Curia (or Senate House). In archaic times, this meant the Curia Hostilia (named for the third Roman king, Tullus Hostilius: inset, 18), on the site of which the Church of Santi Luca e Martina (inset, 16) now sits. It was enlarged by the dictator Lucius Cornelius Sulla in 80 BC (destroying the Comitium), then rebuilt by his son Faustus Cornelius

**Figure 1.2:** The Curia Julia on the Roman Forum, with the dome of Santi Luca e Martina behind it, and the footprint of the Basilica Paulli-Aemelia and ruins of the Templum Pacis in the foreground.

Sulla after it was destroyed by riots in 52 BC, then converted into a temple by Julius Caesar during his dictatorship. The Curia Julia (inset, 17) in today's Forum Romanum (figure 1.2) is a twentieth-century restoration of the building Caesar did not live to see finished, which was absorbed into the seventh-century Church of Sant'Adriano al Foro. (In *The Roman Forum*, David Watkin directs visitors to the doors of St John Lateran for an encounter with the original doors of the Julian Curia, which were moved there in the seventeenth century.)

Tradition accords seven men the title of King of Rome. Romulus (753–715 BC) was followed by Numa Pompilius (715/16–673/2 BC), who understood the importance of a well-ordered pantheon and is credited with organizing Rome religiously. Next comes the aforementioned Tullus Hostilius (673–642 BC), then Numa's grandson, Ancus Marcius (642–617 BC). Three Tarquin kings follow: Lucius (616–579 BC), Servius Tullius (578–535 BC) and Lucius Tarquinius Superbus (534–510 BC) – all dates being tenuous to one extent or another. The ascendancy of the purportedly Etruscan Tarquins to the throne is an important indicator of the slow cultural assimilation into Rome of its religiously and artistically advanced neighbours. The son-in-law of his predecessor and son of a servant, the penultimate king, Servius, is portrayed by history as a popular ruler whose power, like that of Romulus, came from the people rather than the Senate (contrivances notwithstanding). Rome's earliest defensive wall (on which, more below) honours him in name, recognizing his importance in defining Rome as a city for the Republic that would shortly follow. His Rome was cosmopolitan, even as it remained anchored in its identity to legend; it was a Rome defined *as Rome* in its own time, a matter of intentions and destiny over circumstance and evolution.

The tyranny of his successor, Tarquinius Superbus (Tarquin the Proud), ended the rule of kings. His reign began with the assassination of Servius and was cut short, in turn, by a popular uprising led by a coalition of four senators. It was born in violence and ended thusly. But this violence also gave birth to a growing awareness of what Rome had the potential to be, which was seized upon by patricians and plebeians alike. Toppling their monarchy, Romans took up a form of self-rule that was something between a democracy, an oligarchy led by the patrician class, and a theocracy. The Senate was led by jointly appointed consuls (originally called *praetors*), who were elected each year by the *comitia centuriata* (Centuriate Assembly) and whose appointment was in each case confirmed by the *comitia curiata* (Curiate Assembly). To all intents, the consuls had the power once held by the kings who preceded them, and were responsible for the protection and sound management of the Republic.

While much of the history of these first centuries was centred in and around the Forum, the force and momentum of Rome in its age of empire were such that very few buildings and structures of the regal and republican times survived that later epoch. The *Lapis Niger* (Black Stone: inset, 13) is an exception. Dating to the first century BC, it covers over what some believe to have been the grave of Romulus, but which seems more likely to have been a shrine to the fire god Vulcan, named the Vulcanal. Whatever the facts of the matter, these pasts are long buried and their cyphers largely closed to us – certainly to the casual visitor, and in some cases to the specialist. The Palatine contains a number of artefacts of archaic domestic life, but like everything else one might encounter there, these sites demand an archaeological imagination – often jollied along by twentieth-century reconstructions.

It is in and around the Forum – in the valley and on the surrounding hills – that we discover the greatest density of Rome's monumental ancient history. The corollary of Augustus' claim to have bequeathed a marble city is that the city of bricks he inherited was almost entirely overwritten, lending form and purpose to what followed in the imperial era, while leaving nothing but the faintest traces on the surface. It is typical of the problem that en route to the oldest traces of its human occupation one encounters a part of the Farnese Gardens (inset, 28) on the Palatine – only to find that this garden is no longer the product of a seventeenth-century antiquarian impulse but has been curated by twentieth-century hands to better represent the horticulture of antiquity.

To approach the history of Rome's first centuries – to wander, that is, the Forum, the Palatine and the Capitoline as Rome's archaic focus, or the Quirinale, Trastevere and, later, the Aventine as it expanded over time – is to walk a fine line between what we can glean from works of contemporary scholarship and reconstructions over many centuries and what we can learn from the historians of the late republican centuries and the years of empire – with their combination of chronicle, tradition and myth. In *Early Rome and Latium*, Christopher Smith reminds us that there is no 'stratigraphy' of myth – one cannot dig through it, like an archaeologist, in search of evidence.[5] But a lack of evidence is not, in itself, basis for disproof. In the study and experience of a city soaked in legend, there is always a risk of not taking seriously something from the realms of tradition that might turn out to have substance. Recalling the discovery of what was possibly the Lupercal cave, a proposition advanced by archaeologist Andrea Carandini at the end of the 1980s serves to reinforce this point.

On the basis of his findings on the Palatine, Carandini argues the case for an original king and an original wall dating to the middle of the eighth century: an historical Romulus who demarcated and defined Rome as a city – an *urbs*, in spirit if not scale. The evidence may not support the traditional founding year of 753 BC, but Carandini insists that a founding gesture was made on the twenty-first day of one eighth-century April. This act was less defensive than spiritual, marking out the *pomerium*: a boundary that consecrated the proper and sanctified territory of the city. In the time of the Republic, a general lost his military authority by crossing the *pomerium* into the city; a divine portent lost its significance by crossing its threshold in departure; and tribunes (the five to ten plebeians appointed to represent pleb interests in the Senate) could only exercise their authority therein. Rome could (and would, eventually) hold sway over any land it could acquire (as *ager publicus*, or Roman land – more often than not held in private hands, and extending to provinces and colonies). It, however, required great ceremony to change the *pomerium*.

Carandini's interpretation of this discovery invited controversy, being a question of ancient postholes (inset, 32) that supported a coincidence of fact and myth speaking 'of something emerging from nothing'.[6] Whatever might have happened, at whose hands and when, of that much we can be certain.

## The Servian Wall

That which emerged was, before long, defined and defended by city walls. This Rome was no longer limited to the Roma quadrata that might once have described the first flowering of this city. This later, fourth-century BC wall contained a mature city – the largest on the Italian peninsula – that would soon come to exceed its own limits. Long replaced by the Aurelian Wall, which remains very much in evidence, the Servian Wall is largely destroyed, surviving merely as fragments along its ancient path. The earlier wall was long held in some quarters to be an extension of that built by Romulus, in which case the wall grew together with the city. By the end of the sixth century, according to Livy, Rome comprised of four tribal regions within the city – *urbs et capitolium*: the Suburana, Esquilina, Collina and Palatina, all named after topographical features, along with the Capitoline as Rome's citadel and religious centre – and twenty-six regions beyond, making for a total of thirty tribal areas gathered under Rome's banner. Livy relates how Rome's defences were critically challenged in what some historians call the Battle of the Allia and others the Gallic Catastrophe in around 387 BC – a Senone invasion that saw Rome retreat to the Arx, emerging bruised, but intact. Tradition casts the construction of the Servian Wall, from 378 BC, as a response to this event.

We might well blame Fabius Pictor for the coincidence of this story (known largely thanks to his stylus and its influence on Livy) with the fourth-century BC firming up of details around the stories of Aeneas, Romulus and Remus – a long moment from which Rome emerged as a force underpinned by myth and chronicle. Building the Servian Wall meant that the Romans could stay in Rome rather than having to relocate elsewhere. Like Rome's myths, the wall is a form of self-confirmation. Over the course of the next century, a suddenly land-hungry Republic would subjugate much of the Italian peninsula in the Samnite Wars. From this base, Rome would conduct war against Carthage and Greece in the third and second centuries BC. It may seem convenient to locate in this episode a moment of introspection and pre-emptive defence before Rome set about asserting itself throughout Italy and the Mediterranean. This, though, is what Livy, after Fabius, suggests, and they therefore imbue the wall with greater meaning for a reinvigorated Roman Republic.

Depending on your means of arrival into Rome, the remnants of the Servian Wall – the fourth-century BC wall, that is – could be one of the first things you see. Immediately outside Termini station, there are two sections of the *agger* (embankment) wall visible in the Piazza del Cinquecento ([main, 7], and another [main, 8] sits alongside the McDonald's in the station's underground shopping level). (Archaeologists have also located another small section underneath platform 24 [main, 9] – at which travellers from the airport at Fiumicino arrive on the Leonardo Express.) Heading south, there is a fragment in the Piazza Manfredo Fanti (main, 12), a couple of blocks from the station, in the gardens in front of the nineteenth-century aquarium (main, 13). Another piece can also be found underneath the small church of Santi Vito, Modesto e Crescenzia (main, 15, which dates to at least the ninth century), alongside the incongruously Neo-Gothic church of Sant'Alfonso de' Liguori (main, 14, designed by Scotsman George Wiley in the 1850s); and yet another in the fabric of the Auditorium of Maecenas (on the Largo Leopardi [main, 21]) at the top of the Esquiline hill.

Some distance around the circuit, at the base of the Aventine hill and a quick walk from the Porta San Paolo ([main, 32], in the later Aurelian Wall), two sections sit alongside the via di Sant'Anselmo (main, 30), commencing in the Piazza Albania and including a section of the wall containing a defensive arch. An underground section on the Vico Jugario (main, 22: historically the Vicus Jugarius, leading into the Forum Romanum) once protected the base of the Capitoline hill; two courses of the *tufo giallo* (yellow stone) in which sections of it were built can be found on the roundabout on the Largo Magnanapoli, under the shadow of the medieval Torre Milizia, in whose grounds a number of other stones have been found, and below the raised gardens of the Villa Aldobrandini. In a neighbourhood dominated by ministry buildings (which, naturally, have been constructed on top of other traces of the wall), two decent-sized remnants flank the via Giosuè Carducci (main, 5) shortly after it meets the via Piedmonte.[7]

For both specialists and visitors, this is very much a matter of trying to imagine the whole from well-dispersed parts. The path of the Servian Wall may not be particularly interesting in itself, but it becomes so the moment we start to think of the extent of fourth-century BC Rome captured within its defences. At the dawn of the Republic, however, Rome turned its back on the Tiber and its western banks (thereby excluding the Vatican plane and hill and the fourteenth Augustan *rione*, or neighbourhood, of Trastevere and the Janiculum), going no further south than the Aventine.

At this time, Rome occupied the high ground, for which the river offered little by way of natural defensive support. That it was small enough to get around on foot can be confirmed even today, offering a study in contrasts with the sprawling metropolis of the twentieth and twenty-first centuries. Regardless of whether or not that first furrow was laid in the earth at the base of the Palatine in 753 BC, or whether the city's defences expanded systematically to encompass the increased extent of regal and republican Rome, at some point in the first decades of the fourth century BC the city of Rome (and the idea of the city bound up in it) took shape within and by means of this wall. It offered a yardstick for what followed, and in this its legacy has long survived.

## A City of Seven Hills

A tour of the path of the Servian Wall helps us to appreciate the distance Rome has travelled as a city. There is a remarkably rich history contained within it, matched, indeed exceeded, by what would come to take place beyond this first impression of the city. We now turn away from the very edges of the early republican city to its defining topography. This offers another way to regard the early republican city and a geography long occupied by the peoples who together realized Rome, and which shaped the city in the first centuries of its existence as such. It is exceedingly difficult, encountering Rome for the first time, to tease apart its layers, especially when monuments of great antiquity continue to shape the city over time.

A map published by the German historian Gustav Droysen in 1886 describes something of the problem encountered by anyone confronted by the image of 'Ancient Rome' (figure 1.3). He superimposes the two key lifetimes of Roman antiquity – the republican Rome bound by the Servian Wall and the imperial Rome that quickly exceeded it – and flattens half-a-millennium's worth of construction and erasure into one, practically homogeneous image of a developed but distant epoch in the city's history. In this it

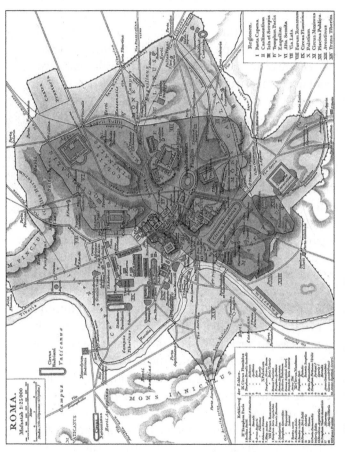

**Figure 1.3:** Gustav Droysen, Map of Rome, *Allgemeiner Historischer Handatlas* (1886).

is typical of maps of Roman antiquity, which reflects, in turn, the typical experience of one not versed in the detail of Rome's archaeological remains. It is telling that the first-century AD Flavian Amphitheatre – the Colosseum – occupies, almost with natural authority, the centre of an ancient city defined by walls that never contained this structure. Very little of what was once bounded by the Servian Wall remains as a touchstone for an encounter with this historical epoch.

Where architecture and infrastructure can fall as easily as they rise, topography tends to win out in the longevity stakes. One configuration of Rome's seven hills is neatly gathered within the Servian Wall in Droysen's image. He depicts the sparsely populated Aventine – covered as it was in lowly *insulae* (apartments, or tenements) rather than lofty *domii* (atrium houses) – and the Palatine packed with temples and aristocratic dwellings. Between them lies the mammoth ancient racing circuit of the Circus Maximus, dating to the sixth century BC and surviving as a vacated imprint on which one can still freely walk. Its long axis extends south–east to meet the start of the famed via Appia and north–west to encounter the Forum Boarium and the mouth of the Cloaca Maxima (main, 24), the city's principal sewer, draining Rome's flood-prone valleys of their excess water.

The Forum Boarium (main, 23) was a large cattle forum and predated the Emporium (main, 29), which was built in the second century BC, serving as the city's main river port. Two temples still stand on the river-edge of this site (opposite Santa Maria in Cosmedin and its famous Bocca della Verità, Mouth of Truth): the Round Temple, perhaps one of several on this site dedicated to Hercules; and the Temple of Portinus, the god of the harbour. Around the edges of this forum the Capitoline, Palatine and Aventine hills rose up high above the Tiber to define Rome's western edge. From south to north, the Caelian, Esquiline, Viminal and Quirinal hills form an arc that captures the city from the east. The Quirinal, northernmost of these, may have been absorbed into an expanding Rome as early as the sixth century through the integration of the Romans and Sabines.

Much is made of the famed hills of Rome, but to the extent that they remain part of today's topography, they are far less pronounced than they were two millennia ago, with centuries of infilling, levelling and drainage robbing the city skyline of the drama they once offered. We can make a best guess at the original seven invoked – which differ from the *montes* that give name to the archaic celebration of the Septimontium – but this risks making a modern approximation of something that changed in composition as parts of the city changed level over time. Hazards of historical error notwithstanding, to move from one hill to the other is both relatively easy and rich with distractions, offering a direct experience of the scale of the city of Rome twenty-five centuries ago.

Given the antiquity of the traces of civilized life still to be found upon them, the Palatine is a clear contender for being one of the seven hills, as is the Capitoline, and we have already spent time on both. The peak of the Aventine can be reached today by following via Santa Sabina (main, 28), named for the fifth-century Dominican basilica, which terminates with the priory church of the Knights of Malta (main, 27). Extensive public gardens cover the shallow Caelian hill (Monte Celio), including those of the sixteenth-century Villa Mattei, now called the Villa Celimontana (main, 26); and the Basilica of Santi Giovanni e Paolo (main, 25), originally dating to the end of the fourth century AD. Further north, the slope extending north–east from the Colosseum through the archaeological site around the Neronian Domus Aurea (main, 19, now open after extensive restoration works) leads to the site of the Baths of Trajan (main, 20) on the mound of the Esquiline hill. Heading north, via Merulana leads to the fifth-century Papal Basilica of Santa Maria Maggiore and, down via Cavour (main, 11), to Termini and (sitting before it) the Baths of Diocletian (main, 6). These baths occupy the juncture of two historical ridges now effectively separated by via Nazionale: the Viminal hill, staked out by the imposing Palazzo del Viminale (main, 10); and the Quirinal, now dominated by the palace and its extensive gardens (main, 4).

A tour of what is left of the Servian Wall might prove disappointing to the reader keen for a strong sense of what fell under Rome's urban dominion at the moment of its republican coming of age. For one thing, beyond some street patterns that continue to respond to topography and the wall itself, even in its absence, there is very little to which you might attach your gaze. Even the visual spectacle of the hills has been dialled down over the centuries as various hollows have been filled by means of public works or built up as successive layers of construction recalibrated the city's ground plane in its most heavily populated areas – flattening hilltops and filling in valleys. (One of the more iconic demonstrations of this is Giovanni Battista Piranesi's eighteenth-century depiction of the half-buried Arch of Septimius Severus [inset 12] in the Forum Romanum – a matter not of subsidence, but of the city floor rising around it over time.) For another thing, as a modern metropolis and a major European capital, Rome now effortlessly exceeds its historical boundaries, so that the logic of its first circuit wall fails to impress upon us an image beyond that of a lost city intermingled with the footings of the modern world. It is, nonetheless, possible to stand unambiguously beyond the city of Rome, as it was then defined: cross the Tiber to Trastevere or the Vatican; descend the broad stairs of Michelangelo's Campidoglio and head north or west into the plane of the Campo Marzio; climb the Pincean hill to visit the Villa Borghese or follow the via Veneto down to the Piazza Barberini. In the middle of the fourth century BC, none of this is yet Rome.

Well beyond the city's republican borders (and a decent metro ride away from the historical centre) is the neighbourhood now called EUR, after the Esposizione Universale that was planned for 1942 (E42), although never staged. There, in the Museo della Civiltà Romana (Museum of Roman Civilization), is a model made in 1994 of the city at the end of the regal period that will have seemed quite recognizable to Romans born in the time of the Republic: rising dramatically above the plane of the flood-prone Campus Martius to show the *urbs* as a thing apart (figure 1.4). Its focus, though, its centre of sorts, is the valley between the Capitoline, the Palatine and the southern spur of the Quirinal. By moving to this spot from the city's edges, we solve at least one of the problems noted above. Standing in the Forum Romanum, we are still unlikely to see anything that might have caught the eye of someone in the fourth century BC, or indeed the second century BC. However, in all senses, the Forum Romanum is – and was for a thousand years – the centre of this city, and to that centre we now return.

### *The Forum Romanum*

David Watkin's book on *The Roman Forum* has no obvious rival in its understanding of both the lay of the Forum Romanum and the complexity of this site, and it serves as an excellent companion to any visitor there.[8] The Forum is a scene that can, in a sense, be stratified. With the right tools and a properly calibrated imagination, the clock can be reset to see along the length of its thoroughfare the way it

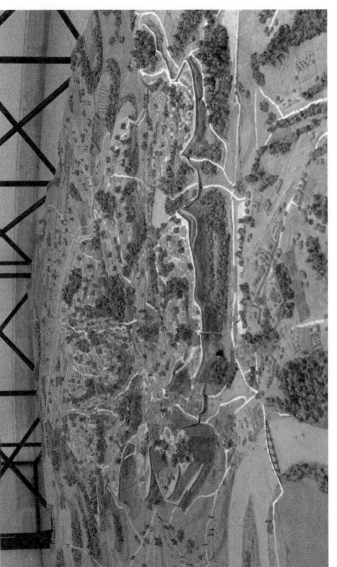

**Figure 1.4:** Lorenzo Quilici, *Model of Archaic Rome* (1994), Museo della Civiltà Romana, Rome.

might have been at the start of the Republic, or at the time of Hannibal's incursions into Italy, or the height of Rome's imperial might, or into the medieval and modern epochs. Few of us, though, have either the tools or the imagination necessary to reconstruct those scenes as they were, and so the Forum can come off as simply a big pile of history. Which it is. While the various layers of the Forum can be (and have been) recovered through excavation and documentation, it has been a setting of perpetual change, responding both to the amassing of events and structures and to the way each successive present moment chooses to celebrate, curate or ignore the various pasts that have been gathered upon it.

As we will see below, four temples were built in this public thoroughfare before the death of Julius Caesar, but like the fragments of the Temple of Castor and Pollux (inset, 24), with their distinctive and conspic-uous set of three Corinthian columns, their fabric, where it endures at all, dates not to republican but to imperial times. The Forum changed markedly and without remorse over the course of its life, letting those buildings and institutions no longer needed by Rome slide into obscurity and disrepair. This presents for those specialists who have sought to represent the history of this site the problem of isolating one or other layer of its history. Successive generations of antiquarians and archaeologists have sought to strike a balance between a dispassionate knowledge of the remains of the past and an invocation of the world from which they originate, between fragments and the coherent image. In Rome, and in the Roman Forum, religion and worship underwent considerable and definitive change. The governing institutions that had once been centred there were moved elsewhere. The demands of various building programmes over several centuries denuded many of the Forum's structures of their marble, gold and bronze – offering a tacit assessment of its symbolic importance for Rome as a whole. Indeed, the Forum as painted by Turner in 1839 was labelled the *Campo Vaccino* in tribute to the cows he saw there, grazing among its monuments. The Forum is not one thing, and is neither singular nor reducible in its significance.

Even so, above or below a shifting ground plane, the Forum retained something of the centuries' worth of alterations, elaborations, reconstructions and reorientations tracking its importance as a site of trade and exchange and of debate and resolution, on so many levels. Any view we might have of the Forum Romanum from *any* vantage today is more likely than not a view that takes the era of empire as its datum – the years, that is, commencing with the plans of Julius Caesar to restore those monuments showing their age (realized, in many cases, by his successor) and to extend the territory of the original Forum into new sites better able to cope with the grand scale of trade and exchange that accrued to a Rome serving as capital of the world. Our eyes, too, might as easily rest upon structures built eighteen or twenty centuries ago

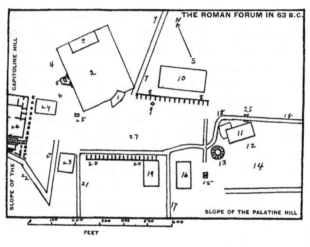

| 1. | Rostra. | 11. | Regia. | 20. | Tabernae veteres. |
| 2. | Comitium. | 12. | Domus Publica. | 21. | Vicus Iugarius. |
| 3. | Senate House. | 13. | Temple of Vesta. | 22. | Clivus Capitolinus. |
| 4. | Basilica Porcia. | 14. | House of the Vestals. | 23. | Temple of Saturn. |
| 5. | Carcer. | 15. | Lacus Juturnae. | 24. | Temple of Concord. |
| 6. | Basilica Opimia. | 16. | Temple of Castor. | 25. | Altar to Volcanus. |
| 7. | Argiletum. | 17. | Vicus Tuscus. | 26. | Tabularium. |
| 8. | Tabernae argentariae (novae) | 18. | Via Sacra. | 27. | Lacus Curtius. |
| 9. | Sacellum Cloacinae | 19. | Basilica Sempronia. | 28. | Fornix Fabianus. |
| 10. | Basilica Fulvia et Aemilia | | | | |

**Figure 1.5:** 'The Forum as Cicero Saw It', annotated plan by Walter Dennison, 1908.

as fall upon twentieth-century tributes to monuments known but lost to time.

If *The Roman Forum* helps with the overview, we can read a brief and century-old essay by the classicist Walter Dennison to imagine what the orator Cicero might have seen of the Forum in the year of his consulship, 63 BC (figure 1.5). This is the year in which Cicero exposed from the Rostra the intentions of one

Lucius Sergius Catilina (or Catiline) to overthrow the Republic by inciting a popular uprising against the aristocratic Senate. This essay's own relative antiquity means that it needs to be checked against more recent archaeological studies of the Forum's contents (as documented in Claridge's *Oxford Archaeological Guide* or the Touring Club guide *Roma*[9]), but questions of accuracy notwithstanding, it makes for a pleasant read even while taking a break from walking the Forum itself – sketching out an alternative, older Forum than the one we might be tempted to attribute to the Roman Republic on first impressions alone.

As we can quickly gather, the Forum was much developed in Cicero's time from the earliest acts of draining the valley to establish the Comitium in archaic times. The oldest of its structures, dating to the rule of kings, are the Carcer (or Mamertine Prison inset, 11; Denn., 5, of which a trace remains on the edge of the Capitoline), the structures under the *Lapis Niger*, the Temple of Vesta (inset, 25; Denn., 13; visible today, in part, as a twentieth-century reconstruction) and the Regia (inset, 26; Denn., 11). The last of these was once the most significant building on the Forum. It originally housed the king, but during the Republic (and thus in 63 BC) it came to serve as the office of the *pontifex maximus* – the chief officer of Rome's religions, which were in turn represented by the Collegium Pontificum. (This was a position to which Julius Caesar was elected in 63 BC.) The Temple of Vesta, with its associated housing for the Vestal

Virgins, and, in front of it, now in outline, the Regia both sat alongside Rome's oldest and most ceremonially significant street, via Sacra (inset, 22; Denn., 18).

Cicero addressed his fellow citizens from the Rostra, at the edge of the paved area of the Comitium and the Curia Hostilia. Cicero's oratory would have reached his audience in a moment in which, as Dennison puts it, 'Roman citizens still had a personal share in the business of state, and republican forms had not yet lost their meaning.'[10] In this same part of the Forum, at the base of the Capitoline hill, the Temple of Concord was raised during the consulship of Lucius Opimius in 121 BC (since largely replaced by the first-century AD Temple of Concordia Augusta: inset, 9). (Lucius is notorious for ordering the execution of three thousand supporters of Gaius Sempronius Gracchus without trial following a mass conflict on the Aventine over Gaius' defeated tilt that same year at the consulship.) A fire in 210 cleared the way for a series of new buildings that Cicero would have seen, including what was originally the Basilica Fulvia (179 BC) and later the Basilica Aemelia (or Basilica Paulli, dating to 55–34 BC: inset, 20; Denn., 10), which first served as a market hall, the outline of which is quite visible alongside the restored Curia.

This basilica occupied a site that had been used by butchers in the early years of the Republic and bankers from the fourth century BC onwards, and it was one of the first four basilicae of the Forum:

Cato's Basilica Porcia (inset, 15; Denn., 4) is the oldest of these, dating to 184 BC, and the Basilica Fulvia, first completed five years later, is in its final form the most intact, although Alaric's Visigoth conquest of the city in AD 410 left little to boast over; the Basilica Sempronia (inset, 23; Denn., 19) was built by Tiberius Sempronius Gracchus in 169 BC and the Basilica Opimia (inset, 10; Denn., 6) in 121 BC. The Basilica Aemelia was separated from the Comitium by the Argiletum (inset, 19; Denn., 7), a street extending north to east from the Forum to Subura – a poorer district known for its vice (hence the themes of the 2015 film by Stefano Sollima that takes its name). Of the character of the Forum in that period, Dennison offers these thoughtful conjectures:

It is probable then that the Forum of 63 BC had a plain, perhaps antiquated, look and its structures showed but little influence of the elegant architectural forms of Greek models. Moreover, the buildings were comparatively few and not lofty, their small proportions being somewhat accentuated by the elevated situation of the temples and the newly erected Tabularium [records office: inset, 7; Denn., 26] on the Capitoline and the private residences of the Roman aristocracy [like that of Cicero himself] on the edge of the Palatine. Ruins of the Roman Forum of this period would impress us in much the same way perhaps as do the plain stucco-covered walls and columns of the forum at Pompeii today.[11]

It was not, then, the highly adorned, decorated and crowded precinct it became from the 40s (BC) onwards, after Julius Caesar returned from Gaul and his truncated dictatorship paved the way for Rome's rule by an emperor rather than its senators. In its more modest form, the Forum allowed, however, for the Quirites (or Roman citizens) to gather and conduct business and politics of all sorts, to participate in games, to hear speeches and partake in debate, and to engage in civic and religious ceremonies. Along the northern and southern edges of the Forum were market stalls (the *tabernae novae* and *tabernae veteres* – new and old stalls – respectively). The area between the Temple of Concord and the Regia was relatively open.

Alongside the Regia was the home of the *pontifex maximus*, the Domus Publica, which explains why his office later extended into the Regia. Alongside the Temple of Vesta was a basin capturing the spring where the sons of Leda appeared after the Battle of Lake Regillus and Rome's victory over the Latin League in 496 or 499 BC: Castor, born to the Spartan king Tyndareus, and Pollux to Zeus; both, therefore, siblings of Helen of Troy and Clytemnestra. Their appearance auspiciously marked a victory in what would have otherwise been a very short-lived Republic. Beside it was a comparatively humble temple in their honour (originally dedicated in 484 BC), already rebuilt twice by Cicero's day and later overbuilt by Tiberius after a fire late in the first century BC. In the face of ruination, the three remaining columns of this later, imperial temple to Castor and Pollux have been standing their ground since the fifteenth century. Spanning via Sacra at the site of the Regia (and, today, the baroque church of San Lorenzo in Miranda [inset 21], which incorporates part of the second-century Temple of Antonius and Faustina), an arch once marked the victory of the general, consul (and dictator) Quintus Fabius Maximus over the Allobroges in 121 BC.

Turning back towards the Capitoline hill would have afforded a view of the Temple of Saturn (inset, 8; Denn., 23) on the site of cult worship dating to the start of the fifth century BC. After Christianity was regularized and pagan worship criminalized at the end of the fourth century AD, the old and new ways were reconciled and the mid-December celebrations of Saturnalia made their way into those of Christmas. What we now see is a fourth-century act of aristocratic resistance: built in honour of Saturn at a time when Rome was turning Christian within a mere generation of the moment when worship of Saturn would be rendered illegal. The Treasury was kept in this temple, under the guard of the Senate, and this was the building breached by Julius Caesar upon his return to Rome. Continues Dennison:

> Looking up toward the Capitoline Hill one saw the towering Temple of Juppiter [sic] Optimus Maximus on the left and on the *arx*, at the right, the upper portion of the Temple of Juno Moneta [somewhere under the eastern end, most likely, of Santa Maria in Aracoeli (inset, 1), whose steps run away from those

leading to the Campidoglio]; the latter was hidden in part by the Tabularium, or archive hall, recently erected [in 78 BC, under Quintus Lutatius Catulus] on the slope of the Capitoline overlooking the Forum [its walls today embedded into those of the medieval Palazzo Senatorio (inset, 1)].[12]

## From Settlement to City

Concluding his tour of the Forum Romanum (and thus ours), Dennison recalls that Cicero witnessed many changes after his consulship, both to the Forum and to the Republic. Demolition of the Basilica Sempronia and the two rows of *tabernae* made way for grander buildings; works were initiated to replace the Curia Hostilia with a new Curia Julia; and the foundations of the Forum Julii were laid, presaging the diminished importance of the Forum Romanum over the imperial forums as the centre of Roman life. The city nonetheless consolidated around this central part of the city as the setting of its most important commercial, legislative and religious activities.

Over time and with Rome's greatly increased regional authority, its population grew, but its historical patterns tend to follow a straightforward logic: the houses of the powerful gravitated to trade and power, hence the large *domus* constructions that once grouped around the Forum and crept up the slope of the Palatine. The construction of these basilicae in the second century BC replaced a number of sizeable, single-level atrium houses (*domus*) owned by Rome's more powerful families on the slopes of the Palatine and along the via Sacra and other roads leading to the centre of the city, and which had gravitated to the Forum as the place where crucial decisions affecting commerce, government, taxes and foreign relations were regularly taken. Proximity to the Forum, in this sense, was proximity to power. As the population grew, it occupied an expanding urban field, hence the *Lex icilia* allowing plebeian occupation of the Aventine and the concomitant spread of warrens of *insulae* (apartment dwellings) thereupon, and the growing importance, too, of the Campus Martius, especially for migrants.

This was a city of growing stature, and its fabric responded to the need to project a strong presence, commemorate military success, pay tribute to an increasing array of deities and accommodate a population that would, by the second century AD, reach a scale not to be seen again for nearly two thousand years. In the wake of the wars with Carthage and Greece, Polybius was impelled, in his second-century BC *Histories*, to exclaim: 'For who is so worthless or indolent as not to wish to know by what means and under what system of polity the Romans in less than fifty-three years have succeeded in subjecting nearly the whole inhabited world to their sole government – a thing unique in history?'[13] He purportedly dedicated forty volumes to this difficult problem, to which Tacitus, too, turned in his *Annals* of AD 109:

Rome at the beginning was ruled by kings. Freedom
and the consulship were established by Lucius Brutus.
Dictatorships were held for a temporary crisis. The
power of the decemvirs did not last beyond two years,
nor was the consular jurisdiction of the military tribunes of long duration. The despotisms of Cinna and
Sulla were brief; the rule of Pompeius and of Crassus
soon yielded before Caesar; the arms of Lepidus and
Antonius before Augustus; who when the world was
wearied by civil strife, subjected it to empire under
the title of 'Prince'.[14]

Tacitus' summary of these first seven centuries in the
history of Rome is rough and ready but functional
enough, and from the valley of the Forum we now
turn to its conclusion and to Rome's life at the centre
of an empire.

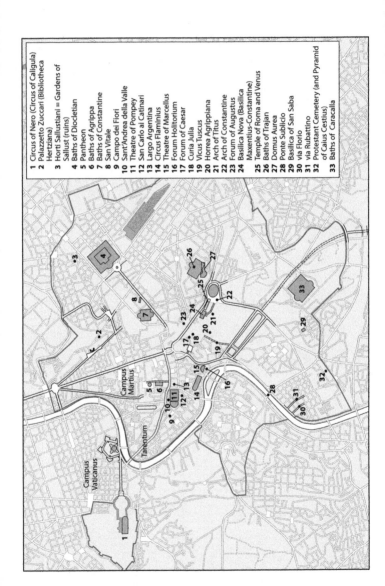

1 Circus of Nero (Circus of Caligula)
2 Palazzetto Zuccari (Bibliotheca Hertziana)
3 Horti Sallustiani = Gardens of Sallust (ruins)
4 Baths of Diocletian
5 Pantheon
6 Baths of Agrippa
7 Baths of Constantine
8 San Vitale
9 Campo del Fiori
10 Sant'Andrea della Valle
11 Theatre of Pompey
12 San Carlo ai Catinari
13 Largo Argentina
14 Circus Flaminius
15 Theatre of Marcellus
16 Forum Holitorium
17 Forum of Caesar
18 Curia Julia
19 Vicus Tuscus
20 Horrea Agrippiana
21 Arch of Titus
22 Arch of Constantine
23 Forum of Augustus
24 Basilica Nova (Basilica Maxentius-Constantine)
25 Temple of Roma and Venus
26 Baths of Trajan
27 Domus Aurea
28 Ponte Sublicio
29 Basilica di San Saba
30 via Florio
31 via Rubattino
32 Protestant Cemetery (and Pyramid of Caius Cestius)
33 Baths of Caracalla

# 2

# *Roma Caput Mundi*

*At the Theatre of Pompey – Augustan Rome – The
Colosseum – Food, Farms and Gardens – The Pantheon
– Bathing and Everyday Life – 'Go Thou to Rome …'*

## At the Theatre of Pompey

Few episodes in the history of Rome are so engrained
into Europe's cultural fabric as the assassination
of Julius Caesar. We know when he died, and at
whose hands (at least one pair of them). Thanks to
Shakespeare, we also probably think we know what he
said just before the end. (HBO's *Rome*, for all its added
colour, does deal with this scene remarkably well.)
But it is easy to forget that while the great dictator was
cremated on the Forum, the site still clearly marked,
he was not killed there. Instead, as the histories have
it, he was assassinated in the Curia outside the theatre
completed in 44 BC by Gnaeus Pompeius Magnus, or
Pompey, styled 'the Great', in the year of his second
consulship. Pompey served Rome on three occasions
as Consul and had been in league with Gaius Julius
and Marcus Licinius Crassus as one of the Amitica:
a senatorial voting bloc, enforced by arms, which
lasted from Caesar's own first consulship (59 BC)

until Crassus was exposed as its weak link, dying at Parthian hands in 53 BC while serving as Governor of Syria. What many euphemistically call the 'irregularities' of Caesar's first consulship prompted his lengthy and fateful sojourns beyond Rome in the 50s (BC), into the Italian north and French south (and beyond, as far afield as Britain), bringing the Gallic regions to heel (at the cost of hundreds of thousands of lives), and acquiring monies, lands and fealty to Rome as he extended the reach of the Republic.

His long-delayed return to Rome in 49 BC provoked a civil war against his former ally Pompey, which Caesar won, and Rome addressed its state of crisis in the traditional manner, setting aside the consulship in favour of Caesar's brief dictatorship (eleven days), followed by another in 48 BC (of indefinite duration), before his own constitutional reforms allowed him to be declared dictator for life in February 44 BC. His travels had taken him to the provinces of western and central Europe and to the Roman lands of northern Africa, including Egypt, upon whose grain Rome relied. Caesar was favourably impressed with the city of Alexandria, against which Rome fared poorly by comparison, and he returned determined to raise its public buildings and forums to a standard befitting Rome's place in the world. He got many such works underway and took extensive action to repair the economic damage of civil war. His authoritarianism, however, ultimately undermined the offices of consul and tribune – both of which Caesar, as dictator, had taken for himself, these being the sacrosanct offices on which, in balance, republican governance had long relied. Caesar's life-long dictatorship was not blessed with longevity – ultimately being shorter than both his first and second spells as dictator – and he met his fate near Pompey's theatre within a month of its proclamation.

The site of the theatre (11) is on the edge of the Campus Tiberinus or Campus Martius and was established alongside four temples dating from the fourth to the second centuries BC (figure 2.1). Like much of the city, Pompey's complex has been overbuilt again and again for many centuries, but its imprint on the city has

**Figure 2.1:** Italo Gismondi, *Model of Rome in the Age of Constantine* (1933–7), detail centred on the Theatre of Pompey.

endured regardless. The semi-circular plan of the theatre itself is clearly legible on the third-century Severan Plan of Rome, otherwise called the *Forma Urbis Romae*. This part of the *Forma Urbis* is now in the Capitoline Museums, but its marble panels were long affixed to the wall of what is now Santi Cosma e Damiano on the Forum Romanum, which once formed part of the imperial-era Temple of Peace. (The Temple of Romulus, which was converted into this church, is dedicated not, as might seem obvious, to Rome's founder, but rather to the deified son of the fourth-century emperor Maxentius.) Pompey's temple is legible, too, in the semi-circular form of the city block wrapped around via di Grotta Pinta in the fabric immediately to the east of the Campo dei Fiori (9), its impressive footprint now bounded north and south by the two baroque churches of Sant'Andrea della Valle (10) and San Carlo ai Catinari (12). You can eat in restaurants and take a hotel room on the site it once occupied.

Over time, the city square under which the earlier republican temples sat became better known by the tower built there, allegedly by the twelfth-century antipope Anacletus II, and which was named for the (now French) city of Strasbourg, or Argentoratum – hence Largo Argentina (13). Demolition on the Corso Vittorio Emanuele II towards realization of the 1883 Regulatory Plan uncovered sections of the temple complex and it has, from that time on, served as a reminder of the archaeological riches that reside beneath the surface of the city.

The Theatre of Pompey was Rome's first theatre. In 55 BC it was inaugurated with five days of live animal hunts; according to Plutarch, hundreds of lions were killed, and innumerable other species imported from Rome's provinces in Africa and Asia were either put to the spear or made to confront other equally entertaining ends. The twenty elephants killed on the final day (wrote Cicero, who was there) presented the crowds with a sobering spectacle; and it was registered as such. As an event it made it into the histories of Pliny, Seneca and Cassius Dio. But its place in history was most firmly secured as the setting of Caesar's final breath: in the Curia, at the entrance to the theatre, where games were being staged and where senatorial business was being conducted. That it should have been here in particular was Caesar's own doing. His building programme on the Forum to raise Rome to the level of Alexandria included a new Curia building, the Curia Julia (18), as well as the entirely new market adjacent to the Forum Romanum, called the Forum Julii (Forum of Caesar, 17). As noted in the previous chapter, the Curia Julia that we can visit on the Forum today is largely reconstructed, but construction works on the original saw Caesar head for Pompey's theatre that March day, and to his end.

The death of Caesar did not, in itself, flip the switch between republican Rome and imperial Rome. Almost two decades of instability, warfare and co-rule followed, in which Gaius Octavius (Octavian), Marcus Aemelius Lepidus and Marcus Antonius (Mark

Antony) shared, and then fought for, power. After the Battle of Actium in 31 BC, Octavian was the last man standing. The Senate granted Gaius Octavian the titles Princeps and Augustus in 27 BC and declared him Imperator Caesar Divi Filius Augustus, thus initiating the 250-year period of the Roman Principate: rule by a single emperor. Records show that Augustus held the consulate for eleven terms up to 23 BC; it was renewed annually after the Battle of Actium, which for some evidenced a conspicuous exercise in unbridled power in the guise of Rome's republican traditions. The so-called Second Settlement of 23 BC regularized this arrangement to prevent further civil war, granting Augustus his imperium and placing Rome's political, financial and military organs under his authority.

An account of the wars Rome waged to secure its position of undoubted prominence in the ancient world would take us well away from our central subject, but the work done in distant lands to advance Rome's military position and add to its imperial provinces cannot be divorced from Rome itself, as a city, through which the spoils of war and the tributes of peace constantly flowed. By the second century AD, the Roman Empire that Augustus founded extended from Hadrian's Wall in Britain to the confluence of the Tigris and Euphrates rivers in Mesopotamia. Rome projected this power upon its territories, connecting the centre to the edge by means of a system of rule that returned all things, pragmatically and symbolically, to the seat of this power: the city itself.

## Augustan Rome

For Augustus, the Forum Romanum was the centre of this enterprise. We ended the previous chapter standing in the Forum with an eye on its appearance and arrangement at the time of the Republic, which is a little like looking through a test lens at the optometrist that is almost but not quite right for our vision. The shapes are in place, the letters more or less discernible; but it is a struggle. Adjusting our outlook to consider the era of imperial Rome is, by contrast, like flipping the glass over to the correct lens. A great deal occurred between Cicero's denouncement of Catiline in 63 BC and the Second Settlement of 23 BC. The Roman Empire emerges triumphant as a form of rule, relegating the Republic to history – if not those of its ideals on which Rome would continue to trade or those of its institutional structures on which it would continue to rely, especially as they concerned urban and provincial governance. Caesar had set out to renovate Rome to more ably reflect that which it invoked as an idea and as an authority. In time Rome realized these ambitions and the Forum and Palatine hill became replete with tributes to emperors, gods and conquests.

In turning this city of bricks into one of marble, Augustus, especially, pursued Caesar's ambitions, armed with the spoils of two decades of warfare. The Temple of Mars Ultor, marking Octavian's military revenge on Caesar's assassins and the start, therefore, of a sustained campaign that left him alone at the top of the heap, finally without challenge, tellingly dominates the Forum of Augustus (23), which was built many years into his reign. These spoils were matched by growth in the city itself, both in population and in extent, which set the tone for subsequent decades and centuries. Octavian realized the ambitions of his adoptive father in overwriting the comparatively modest monuments of the republican city, including those of the Forum as its traditional ceremonial focus. He oversaw the restoration of older temples and the construction of new structures that left to the city buildings of an unprecedented grandeur.

Octavian completed, as we shall see, many of the projects initiated by Caesar and left unfinished at the time of his assassination, including the new Forum Julii, intended to accommodate the needs of an ever larger city – trade, diplomacy, taxes, offerings – at the centre of an ever-expanding set of territories and colonies. He rebuilt and restored temples that had fallen into disrepair, including (and perhaps even commencing with) Romulus' own Temple of Jupiter Feretrius on the Capitoline. He understood Rome to be an organic, growing *urbs* upon which he superimposed a revised administrative logic that has in some form or other survived to the present day.

Reflecting a way of ordering the city dating to the era of Rome as *urbs et capitolium*, by the end of the first century BC, Augustus had organized Rome's neighbourhoods into fourteen administrative regions (*rioni*), including eight within the Servian Wall and six beyond. They reflected concentrations of economic activity, topography, religious adherence, population and social makeup. Each region was governed by a magistrate who had oversight of legal and religious matters, which were inextricable one from the other. The *rioni* show how the city had outgrown the edges captured by the Servian Wall. What had in the fourth century BC encircled the largest city on the Italian peninsula by the first century (BC, but certainly AD) effectively described an historical centre with an extra-urban sprawl – much as in the relationship today between the Rome captured within the third-century AD Aurelian Wall and all that spills out beyond it into the surrounding suburbs and countryside.

The *rioni* were known initially by their number (each noted on Droysen's map, figure 1.3), but gradually acquired the names, too, of those monuments, roads and topographical features around which they were arranged: Porta Capena (I), named for the gate at the start of via Appia; Caelimontium (II), named like Esquiliae (V), Palatium (X) and Aventinus (XIII) for the area of those hills; Isis et Serapis (III), centred on the lands that would, in time, belong to the fiddling Emperor Nero and on which the Colosseum was later built; Templum Pacis (IV), centred on the forum built by Vespasian (the Temple of Peace) and hence named long after Augustus' reign; Alta Semita (VI), including the Julian Gardens of Sallust (named for the historian who acquired them from Caesar, 3) between the Pincian and Quirinal hills, as well as the Baths (much later) of Constantine (7) and Diocletian (4); via Lata (VII) on the Campus Martius, named for the street that would in time become via del Corso; Forum Romanum (VIII), Circus Flaminius (IX) and Circus Maximus (XI), which all speak for themselves; Piscina Publica (XII) on the Piccolo Aventino, where the Basilica of San Saba now sits (29); and the sole *rione* west of the Tiber, Trans Tiberium (XIV, modern-day Trastevere, its plane giving way to the Janiculum) – once an Etruscan settlement but long integrated into the city proper.

The area of the Campus Martius, in particular, took on greater importance in the reign of Augustus, which was reflected in his decision to build his mausoleum there, and consolidated by sustained building in the two following centuries. Towards the end of the first century AD, Domitian founded a stadium, sometimes called the Circus Agonalis, on the site now called the Piazza Navona, hence the name of the baroque Church of Sant'Agnese in Agone), which served as one of several venues catering to the Roman *ludi*, or games. To the east of the Stadium of Domitian, Nero had two decades earlier built the baths that would (today) abut the piazza in front of the Pantheon (5) – the massive domed structure first built under the efforts of Octavian's close friend and son-in-law, Marcus Agrippa, in the years immediately after he had been declared Augustus.

Agrippa was one of the most prolific builders of the Roman Empire, both within Rome and beyond, and he himself constructed baths at what is now the rear of the Pantheon, in the direction of the modern Largo Argentina, on his own extensive extra-mural lands. It can be easy to forget that monuments did not simply pile up one on top of the other in the Campus Martius across antiquity, but were subject to fires, floods and earthquakes over the centuries. This entire plane is, in many respects, a palimpsest: overwritten and overwritten again across many years. The fire that destroyed Agrippa's original Pantheon in AD 80 was the fire, too, that cleared the land on which Domitian would, as part of his rebuilding programme, construct his own stadium. All of these structures, of course, sat firmly outside the city walls (and indeed the sacred *pomerium*). But within the walls of these buildings and across the Campus Martius, Rome's foreign communities and their gods were slowly absorbed, shaping the city's culture, its arts and, significantly, its pantheon.

The broad, flat topography of the Campus Martius was well suited to the Stadium of Domitian, just as it had for more than three centuries served the Circus Flaminius (14) in the lozenge of land between what is today the Largo Argentina and the northern face of the Capitoline hill. The populist consul Gaius Flaminius Nepos had demarcated the Circus Flaminius for games in 221 BC, and even as it was gradually built in by the expanding city, this site was long used for equestrian activities and other public entertainments. Importantly, it was one of the earliest formal sites on which were staged the republican Secular Games, or Ludi Saeculares, held on an unoccupied and religiously significant part of the Campus called the Tarentum, west of the Piazza Navona. This area gave the games the oldest names by which they are now known, specifically the Ludi Tarentini, or the Taurian Games (Ludi Taurii).

They originated as an offering to the deities Dīs Pater (god of the underworld) and Proserpine (goddess of fertility) – Roman gods with counterparts in the Greek pantheon – whose altars were located on the Tarentum. The games were, perhaps, staged first in 348 BC as a Roman adaptation of an Etruscan tradition, and then (with more historical certainty) in 249 and 146. They were intended to be a periodic, indeed generational, festival, with the term *saeculum* corresponding to an irregular period of time that settled at around 110 years by the time of Augustus. On each occasion of these games, Rome paid tribute to those gods on whom its prosperity and good fortune relied. While the games were held occasionally until the third century AD (as Ludi Saeculares), they would later be reincarnated, in a sense, as the papal jubilees instigated by the ill-fated Boniface VIII and reinstated with the papacy's return from Avignon – to which we will turn in Chapter 4.

During the era of Empire, Rome was an authority invoked each time a citizen declared *civis romanus sum* – an appellation granted by Caracalla in AD 212 to all free men and women who lived within its borders. The city itself was a crossroads connecting all of those territories over which it held sway, and on which its might and majesty rested. Games began as a matter of worship and tribute, and even in their most extensive and insistent form were a matter of much greater import than distraction alone: they ensured the cohesion of a society that was anything but naturally coherent. The one million or so people who lived in the city by the end of Augustus' reign may largely have been Romans, but they were not, by and large, *from Rome*. Romans were Spanish, Arabian, Levantine and British, and the city served as a material corollary to the idea conjured up by the name. Rome may not have been the world's only imperial capital, but it was, as a city, for four centuries the capital of a Roman world that acknowledged no legitimate exterior.

In mounting the Secular Games in the summer of 17 BC, Augustus pursued the restitution of the image of the Roman Republic, which had been undermined by the civil wars provoked by the return and then assassination of Julius Caesar. They signalled the continuity of tradition in the face of rupture, connecting the civic values of republican Rome to the Rome of Augustus – and in their memory to the Rome of the emperors who would follow him. The Ara Pacis Augustae is a concrete monument to this moment of stability. As in their conception, the Games remained a religious affair, with daytime and nocturnal offerings to the most ancient of Rome's gods, plays, hunting and chariot racing. By bringing the Roman people together in entertainment and devotion, Augustus also marked a time in which Rome was a city unified and consecrated under its emperor.

## The Colosseum

Returning to the Forum Romanum and following via Sacra away from the Capitoline hill, past the columns marking the site of the Temple of Castor and Pollux and the ancient footprint of the Regia, the ground slopes up towards the first-century AD Arch of Titus (21) – the enormous shell of the Basilica Nova (24) to the left; beyond which ruins of the Temple of Roma and Venus are cloaked in the medieval garb of what is today the Church of Santa Francesca Romana (but which was once called Santa Maria Nova, 25). By now, the view has given way to the monolithic amphitheatre that rises up to dominate the skyline, a striking symbol of the Roman Empire: the Colosseum (figure 2.2).

Technically called the Flavian Amphitheatre, it is named for the late-first-century dynasty that saw it raised: the emperors Vespasian, Titus and Domitian, who collectively ruled from AD 69 to 96. Its distinctive oval plan form occupies the low basin shaped by the Caelean, Esquiline and Palatine hills, built on the sprawling grounds on which Nero realized his vast

**Figure 2.2:** Italo Gismondi, *Model of Rome in the Age of Constantine* (1933–7), detail centred on the Temple of Venus and Roma and the Colosseum.

and luxuriant Domus Aurea after the Great Fire of AD 64 – which had conveniently cleared the site of any obstacles.

Construction on the stadium began under Vespasian in AD 72 and was completed by his son and successor Titus in the year 80. The imposing structure is made of concrete vaults clad in travertine marble clamped together with iron – mammoth quantities of both, and where the marble and iron have fallen or been stripped off and repurposed over time, their absence registers as the pockmarks that spread across its large surface. Four layers of arches, one on top of the other, reach a height of 53 metres and offer a study in the Greek architectural orders of (from the ground up) Doric, Ionic and Corinthian – one order per level in ascending degrees of delicacy, with the top tier decorated with Corinthian pilasters embedded in a continuous wall. More than this, though, it brings together the Greek style of building with embellished columns and the older Roman tradition of building with arches, and hence is one of many instances where the artists, engineers and writers of imperial Rome looked to and absorbed lessons from the highest achievements of the lands and peoples over which it held dominion.

The Colosseum suffered fire damage in 217 following a lightning strike – with reconstruction concluded in 240 and further repairs in the second and third centuries. An earthquake in 433 demanded more repairs still, which carried on into the first years of the sixth century. The last games held there were staged in 435, and the final animal hunts in the 520s. Between the sixth and eighteenth centuries, it housed all manner of functions: housing, workshops, a cemetery and various religious roles for the Christian Church. As it fell (or came loose, one way or another), marble and iron were distributed into any number of live building projects throughout the city. Like many of the ruins of Roman antiquity, its current state owes much to the nineteenth-century efforts to halt its slide into complete ruination.[1]

Estimates vary as to the capacity of the Colosseum, but the consensus settles on around fifty thousand spectators – divided neatly into class groups, with the best views and greatest comforts given to the wealthy. As such, it held around a fifth of the quarter-million capacity the ancient Circus Maximus had reached by the first century AD; used for all manner of games and spectacles over its lifetime, this circus had, by the age of Empire, become particularly famous for its chariot racing. Not the largest of the facilities dedicated to Roman *ludi*, then, the Colosseum was nonetheless a great deal larger than its most significant predecessor, the Theatre of Marcellus (15), which, even so, could still hold around twenty thousand people. (Julius Caesar wanted this new theatre to rival that of Pompey, and Augustus realized Caesar's ambitions after his death, naming it after his own nephew and intended heir.) As noted above, games and spectacles were vital to Roman culture from the earliest moments in the city's history, and its circuses, theatres and amphitheatres were an important focus of civic life. Recall the dramatic chariot race of *Ben-Hur*, set in the reign of Augustus' successor Tiberius. Remember, too, that one of Rome's founding stories, the abduction of the Sabine women, takes place during games hosted by Romulus for the Romans and their neighbouring tribes.

Nothing could compare with Rome at the height of its imperial power and with the Colosseum as the focus of its festivities. In the second-century reign of Marcus Aurelius, 135 legislated days of *ludi* were held. Even after the Roman Empire had split in two and the western capital had moved to Milan (Mediolanum) with the apparatus of the state, Rome's aristocracy ensured the continued supply of games for their people, with historical sources recording 175 days of games in 354 – on one hand, a sure sign of resistance in favour of Roman traditions as Christianity edged out the older faiths; on the other, a sign, perhaps, of the games' role in diverting attentions from matters of arguably greater immediate concern.[2]

The second-century poet Juvenal gave form to a particularly Roman culture of appeasement that centred on games and which saw, too, the wealthy freely distribute food to the populace: *panem et circenses*, bread and circuses. Together these things suggest a culture in which entertainment and nourishment together distracted the citizenry from the horrendous conditions in and under which many lived: eating bread while watching gladiators fight, criminals and traitors meet their fates and animals of amazing variety go to the slaughter.

Beyond this, however, the games were part of a tradition by which *munera* (public gifts) were the domain of individuals rather than the state. Rome was well stocked with facilities to foster generosity of this kind: besides those stadia and circuses in the Campus Martius mentioned above, in the Campus Vaticanus, circuses were named for Hadrian (on the plane behind his mausoleum, Gaius (or Caligula, 1) and Nero that date to the first century AD (and its infamous persecution of Christians); and much later: the small third-century Amphitheatrum Castrense (alongside, today, the pilgrim church of Santa Croce in Gerusalemme), around which the Aurelian Wall would turn.

To host games was to offer something to the city, and early in the life of the Colosseum it was the sole preserve of the emperor to stage games for the people of Rome within its walls.

The Flavian Amphitheatre, then, stands as a reminder of this social facility and its bloody collateral. Curiously, the popular name Colosseum refers not to the size of the structure – colossal though it certainly is – but to the scale of the statue that once stood before it at the entrance to the Domus Aurea. The golden Colossus of Nero was at first thinly disguised as a tribute to the sun-god Sol, or Helios, which after Nero's death in AD 68 was changed to make a more explicit homage to the deity. Built by a Greek sculptor named Zenobius, the Colossus measured between 30 and 35 metres in height, on a par with the famed Colossus of Rhodes, with 7-metre-long spikes extending from its head to depict the rays of the sun. (As a matter of scale, compare the Colossus of Constantine, constructed for the Basilica Nova and surviving as a series of fragments in the Palazzo dei Conservatori: this presiding figure would have been around 12 metres high, barely a third the size of the Colossus of Nero.) More than a century after the end of Nero's reign, it was further altered by Commodus to turn it into a statue of Hercules. The end of Commodus' reign precipitated the Year of the Five Emperors (193), from which emerged the Severan dynasty. This dynasty was founded by the general Septimius Severus, who is commemorated in perpetuity with a major triumphal arch on the Forum Romanum, mentioned in the previous chapter as depicted in an apparently sunken state by Piranesi. Severus may have seen the Colossus rededicated to Sol around the start of the third century. His reign brought about a brief period of stability that descended into the chaos of what has come to be known as the Crisis of the Third Century, from which the Empire barely recovered, and not, in the scheme of things, for very long. As much as the Colossus switched its allegiance in response to the prevailing winds, in itself, and over time, it remained a constant reminder of imperial might.

That is not to suggest that it was something otherwise static. In 126, the Emperor Hadrian saw it relocated to a site today marked by a tree sitting roughly on an axis with the fourth-century Arch of Constantine (22), between the Forum Romanum and the Colosseum. This was to make way for the construction of the impressive joint temple we passed earlier (25), dedicated to the deified Roma (Rome incarnate) and to Venus (mother of Aeneas) on via Sacra – its grandeur now gone, but its footprint still quite legible behind the church that now rests on a part of their foundations. It demands some imagination to picture these structures at their full height – nearly twice that of the nearby Arch of Constantine and within mere metres of the height of the Colosseum. Between the

Temple of Roma and Venus, the Colossus and the Flavian Amphitheatre, not to mention the mile-long colonnade and artificial sea of Nero's Domus Aurea, this was a precinct of very big things. It famously took the strength of twenty-four elephants to move the Colossus the 100 metres, give or take, from its first setting to the next.

Doubling back past the Temple of Roma and Venus, we can turn around and look at the Colosseum through the frame offered by the Arch of Titus (figure 2.3), which was dedicated to Divus (Divine) Titus, and likely, therefore, to have been built sometime after his death in AD 81. A close historical bond exists between these

**Figure 2.3:** Arch of Titus with Colosseum in the background, 1880.

two monuments. The Arch of Titus commemorates the squashed uprising against Roman rule in the province of Judæa that began with insurrection in AD 66 and was ended in 70 (under Titus' command), when the besieged Jewish capital was sacked and plundered and the Second Temple of Jerusalem was destroyed. The riches of Jerusalem, and of the Temple in particular, were then brought to Rome. The reliefs on the Arch of Titus memorably depict a menorah and trumpets in the hands of Roman soldiers, but it is the Colosseum that fittingly dominates the view, since it – more than any other monument – absorbed Jerusalem's spoils. These riches paid for its construction, and the slaves returned to Rome provided the labour that saw it built. The Colosseum stands as one of the most distinctive emblems of Ancient Rome, but as a monument that serves the image of the Roman Empire it also recalls the means by which that empire was built and maintained. Samuel Johnson might well have had the Colosseum in mind when he wrote, 'I know not why any one but a schoolboy in his declamation should whine over the Commonwealth of Rome, which grew great only by the misery of the rest of mankind. The Romans, like others, as soon as they grew rich, grew corrupt; and in their corruption sold the lives and freedoms of themselves, and of one another.'[3]

Despite the longevity of the Colosseum, it was with the Colossus rather than the Amphitheatre that visitors to Rome long associated the Empire's power and prowess. Well after the end of the Western Empire in the fifth century and the Gothic Wars of the sixth, the Venerable Bede could write, 'as long as the Colossus stands Rome stands too; when the Colossus falls, Rome will fall. When Rome falls, so falls the world.'[4] The Colossus did fall eventually, though whether it was destroyed at the hands of foreign invaders or spoliated for new buildings (its materials reused) is a matter of speculation. Close to two thousand years after its construction, however, we can be certain that the Colosseum rather than its namesake now stands for Rome and its Empire.

## Food, Farms and Gardens

The Empire was a great deal more than an embodiment of unbridled ambitions or an unrestrained military impulse. The vast expanse of its lands made for a highly diversified economic base, slave class and trading power that fed Rome's coffers and its peoples. As a city set inland above a marshy plain, its trade relied heavily on the ancient harbour city of Ostia (Antica), at the mouth of the Tiber. While ships arrived into this seaport until well into the life of the Republic, goods destined for Rome travelled some 30 kilometres upriver to be received at the Forum Boarium, to all intents into the commercial centre of the city. Wine, oil, grain, firewood, cloth, granite and marble: all these and more were stored in substantial warehouses (*horrea*) both alongside the river and at strategic trading points within the city – which in its more socially elevated neighbourhoods would have served less to house the dirty cut and thrust of trade than as a market suited to the sensibilities of the gentry.

The partly exposed footprint of the Augustan-era Horrea Agrippiana (20) is an artefact of this commerce. Embedded into the ground alongside the sixth-century Orthodox church of San Teodoro on the western base of the Palatine, it once sat on the important trade thoroughfare of the Vicus Tuscus (19). The remains are Hadrianic rather than Agrippan, a reconstruction of the first-century BC original dating to the later emperor's improvements to the building and its standing in the second century AD. Its central shrine reminds us that the intention of this type of building, like that of so many others, was not purely to serve the pragmatic functions of storage and trade, but to keep the people in good favour with the gods, which would be manifest as commercial and agricultural success. Another example of this kind of structure is the Basilica Nova, which sits imposingly upon a site that for around a century (between the first-century reign of Domitian and the major city fire that occurred in the reign of Commodus, in 191) housed the *horrea piperataria* (pepper or spice warehouses).

While markets located on the inner city trading streets and around the Forum Romanum and the imperial forums long served their shopping public, the city's needs soon rendered the Forum Boarium inadequate as a river port. As early as the start of the second century BC, the area south of the Aventine, outside the city walls in today's Testaccio, was developed as a large urban river port, its complex including warehouses, wharves and shipyards, parts of which having been restored at various times, their ruined fabric absorbed into the twentieth-century buildings of the neighbourhood. The wall ruins visible from via Rubattino (31) and via Florio (30), for instance, likely belong to an enclosed and sloping shipping yard of half a kilometre in length. Traces of storage sheds and markets are likewise visible along the edge of the Tiber, south of the Ponte Sublicio (28). Upstream, the Forum Holitorium (16), or Vegetable Market, negotiated its way from antiquity, through the middle ages and down to the modern era, long occupying a site north of the Forum Boarium near the medieval church of San Nicola in Carcere and Piazza di Monte Savello.

Rome was for a long time a city that fed itself. The surrounding *campagna* was peppered with small landholdings whose harvests were absorbed by the *urbs*; farms for the raising of livestock similarly destined for the packed marketplaces of the city; and aristocratic landholdings in which agriculture in part worked the land to produce olives, grapes, spelt, figs and other crops suited to the region's soil and climate. In the first century BC, the scholar Varro wrote a treatise, *Rerum rusticarum*, *On Farming*, in which the relationship between pragmatism, culture and religion is demonstrably fundamental to the farmer's craft. The agricultural year followed festivities recognizing the role played by all manner of gods, major and minor, in the success of each harvest, while the technical proficiency of the farmer in understanding the needs of each crop, soil type or animal gave the gods something with which to be pleased. Varro accords honour to life on the land over life in the city. It is a more ancient existence and is imbued with a stronger morality. The farms of the Roman *campagna*, and Italy, may have kept Rome well fed for many centuries, but as the city continued to grow and grow, surpassing (at best guess) a million inhabitants at the ancient peak of its population, it was increasingly dependent on importation for even its most basic commodities. In this it had the full extent of the Empire at its disposal.

Where Romans once maintained gardens of various kinds within the city's walls, the urban landscapes of the imperial age were a form of public amenity akin to the Villa Borghese today – no longer the productive gardens that may have occupied the city's edges. The Republican Gardens of Lucullus (Horti Luculliani), for instance, once extended across part of that very site on the Pincean hill. (Its ruins were uncovered during the recent restoration of the seventeenth-century Palazzetto Zuccari, home of the Bibliotheca Hertziana [2], in 2001.) The prized Gardens of Sallust (3), or Horti Sallustiani, occupied part of the now-levelled depression between the Pincean and Quirinal hills. These were landscapes replete with temples and grottos that, as ruins set in arcadian vistas, inspired the painters of the eighteenth and nineteenth centuries –

landscapes of repose rather than toil. And there is, perhaps, something of this caught in their afterlife. Passing into imperial ownership, where they were maintained as public gardens, they fell into disrepair after the fifth-century invasion by Alaric, only to be taken up by the Ludovisi family in the seventeenth century. This estate was eventually developed for the modern city, and the blocks running between via Vittorio Veneto and the Porta Pia were turned into housing for a professional middle class – and realized, on via Veneto, an image of the modern good life so evocatively captured by Fellini.

Ruins of the ancient gardens survive just a short walk from the Porta Pia (down via Servio Tullio off via XX Settembre): a pavilion that would once have had a commanding view of the grounds. Having in the previous chapter found it remarkably easy to move around and through Rome as it was defined in the early centuries of the Republic, it is telling that by the era of the emperors the remains of these vast grounds sit at such a distance from the hustle and noise that would have pervaded the area in and around the markets, docks and shipyards of the Emporium. They offer a study in contrasts that would have been available to Romans even at the city's busiest.

### The Pantheon

A return, at this point, to the Campus Martius is a return to a part of Rome that by the second century AD was thoroughly involved in the life of the city, housing temples, baths and games venues. The city walls had a symbolic role in defining the Roman *urbs*, but the development of lands on which to build saw Rome sprawl beyond its republican defences, which diminished in practical importance with time. Conversely, much could happen here that could not happen inside the *pomerium*. The consul and military general Marcus Agrippa owned a large tract of land on the Campus Martius, and on it sits the Pantheon (5) (figure 2.4): a distinctive and irreducible relic of Rome's imperial past that has for nineteen centuries shaped life around it.

There is some uncertainty as to the original purpose of this building. It was unlikely to have been a temple dedicated to all the gods, as the most common meaning of its name today might suggest. It may have been built as an audience hall dedicated to 'excellence' – another sense of the Greek word *theios*.[5] Perhaps not a temple as such, then, so much as a tribute in stone from Marcus Agrippa in honour of the esteemed qualities of the Emperor Augustus and his clan, the Julii. Agrippa and Octavian had served together as Consuls in 28 and 27 BC and were, by most accounts, friends; indeed, Agrippa had married Augustus' own daughter, now known as Julia the Elder. Historian Adam Ziolkowski goes further, suggesting that Agrippa's Pantheon may have been originally intended to serve the programme of public works initiated by Julius Caesar as part of his intended development of the Campus Martius.[6] Caesar

**Figure 2.4:** Giovanni Paolo Panini, *Interior of the Pantheon, Rome,* ca. 1734.

had planned to build what has come to be known as the Temple of Mars 'in Campo' – dedicated to the god of war, for whom the entire plane was named. The original rectangular structure, more suited to a temple, and a single deity, more suited to Roman practices, make this a plausible possibility.

Originally built after the First Settlement (27–5 BC) – and hence as a monument in the first, tentative years of the Augustan imperium – it burned down a century later in the fire of AD 80. We have already noted Domitian's own prowess as a city-builder, self-styled as an Augustan figure. The Pantheon was first reconstructed under his authority in a works programme that included the completion of the Flavian Amphitheatre and of the stadium that once occupied the Piazza Navona, a short walk to the west of the Pantheon. It did not last long, though. While the two venues for *ludi* survived, Domitian's Pantheon was destroyed in 110 – the result of a fire caused by a lightning strike.

As an emperor, Hadrian was known for being highly involved in the building arts. He appropriately sits alongside Agrippa and Augustus in history as one of the most important figures in the shaping of Rome's imperial landscape, and the traditional claim is that he had a hand in the composition and construction of over thirty structures in Rome alone, including, besides the Pantheon, his own imposing riverside mausoleum (the Mausoleum of Hadrian, or Hadrian's Mole, now called the Castel Sant'Angelo), a sprawling estate from which he governed the Roman Empire and the Temple of Roma and Venus.

A decade or so (and, perhaps, other reconstruction plans) later, Hadrian's frieze bears a tribute to

Agrippa's original Pantheon rather than recognizing Domitian as the author of its first reconstruction, and eschews, of course, any credit due to Hadrian himself: M. AGRIPPA L. F. COS TERTIVM FECIT – Marcus Agrippa, son of Lucius, three times consul, made this. There is no misdirection in this. Hadrian is known for keeping the original dedications on those buildings he restored. In constructing a new 'Pantheon' on its site, though, he made a building that was anything but faithful to the original. Should you stand anywhere in the round drum of today's Pantheon and look towards the door, you would, in effect, be looking *towards* the portico façade of the old Pantheon from completely outside the original building. The rectangular plan of Agrippa's original temple is almost entirely contained by the portico through which you now pass to stand under the present-day Pantheon's impressive dome. It was a different shape, and faced a different direction. The original Pantheon was not exactly small on its own terms, but it would have been dwarfed by its later incarnations.

The bricks of the rotunda are date-stamped AD 118, which is a testament to Hadrian's enthusiasm for building. That date puts the reconstruction of the Pantheon in the second year of his rule, which suggests that he authorized work to begin immediately upon his return to Rome from Syria as emperor. This was the same year in which he began works on what we now call Hadrian's Villa – the luxurious palace at Tivoli in the Roman *campagna* that came to serve as the seat of the Roman Empire. Hadrian's importance for the urban history of Rome is not to be understated. He raised the level of the Campus Martius around the areas dedicated to Augustus and introduced flood-control measures. Like Augustus before him, he renovated many of the temples, including those with which Augustus and his immediate successors had marked Rome's transition from a city-republic to an imperial capital. In doing so, he sought efficiencies in the entire process of procurement and construction and is credited with streamlining the brick industry to realize his ambitions. (It is entirely appropriate, therefore, that the Australian engineers who in 2015 introduced a brick-laying robot that can build a house in just two days named it the 'Hadrian 109'.)

The Pantheon is composed of two distinct parts: a Greek-style portico and the domed drum for which it is famous. The portico is eight columns wide and topped with a triangular pediment. It shows the high regard in which Roman culture of the first and second century AD held the artistic achievements of Periclean Athens and Hellenistic Greece. It goes further than a simple tribute to the Roman penchant for Hellenistic fashions at this time, though, honouring that other signal architectural achievement of Mediterranean antiquity: the Parthenon in Athens. The bases and capitals of the columns of the Pantheon portico were made of marbles quarried at Mount Pentelicus, the same source as had been used for the columns of the Parthenon more than five hundred years earlier.

The granite of the sixteen columns themselves spoke to the Roman Empire's own second-century extent, being imported from the quarries of ancient Syene (modern-day Aswan, on the Nile, more than 1,000 kilometres upriver from Alexandria). The dome, for which the building is rightly famed, is a technically ambitious study in concrete, resulting in a perfect interior hemisphere spanning more than 40 metres. Its coloured marble floors and coffered ceiling give the interior a geometrical regularity.

The oculus at the apogee of the dome spans more than 8 metres. Through it, the action of the sun upon the walls and floor of the Pantheon over the course of the day and year gives rise to the idea that the activities the building witnessed in between its second-century construction and its fourth-century demise as a setting for Roman religious rites may have related to the solar or lunar passage. Another theory has it that the very decision to 'rebuild' Agrippa's temple for a second time was a kind of rhetorical assertion by Hadrian of his right to rule. Agrippa's Pantheon had burned down, arguably reflecting poorly on the reign of Augustus; as had that of Domitian. To build the Pantheon and have it stand would be a proof of sorts that the gods thought well of Hadrian's right to rule. The Vitruvius scholar Indra Kagis McEwen has observed some resonance between the ancient (Etruscan) order of the cosmos and the arrangement of the building into sixteen divisions, in which the opening of the oculus on to the heavens might offer some clue.[7] In placing the Pantheon upon a vast circular foundation, Hadrian founded a *templum* that encapsulated the city on which the Empire rested. Ultimately, though, whether it was intended to mark the passage of the heavenly bodies or to invite the gods to endorse or decry Hadrian's reign, the Pantheon, as it stands, was not destroyed by lightning. And even if it did not survive from the second century to the present unmolested, it remains one of the most awesome legacies of Rome's imperial past.

Over the centuries it was propped up and pared back on a number of occasions. The ground level changed so that it was necessary to descend thirteen steps to enter the Pantheon, a little like the effect of entering San Vitale (8) on via Nazionale. As a Christian church and centre of the neighbourhood's civic life, it was crowded over by market stands and *ad hoc* additions to meet the needs of the Chapter of St Mary and the Martyrs, to the extent that one whole corner of the portico required reconstruction when the sixteenth- and seventeenth-century popes turned their attention towards it. The Chigi pope Alexander VII was even moved to write, in 1656, 'For the third time let's chase that flower seller from in front of the left column of the portico of Santa Maria Rotonda.'[8] In the sixteenth century, two bell-towers were added above the portico to the design of Carlo Maderno (although they were commonly called the 'asses' ears of Bernini'), and while they were eventually removed, they are still visible in nineteenth-century photographs. The bronze in the portico had been repurposed in the early part of the

seventeenth century at the hands of the Barberini pope
Urban VIII. The interior was substantially reworked
under the authority of Alexander VII. Their ambition
was to isolate it from the fabric of the seventeenth-
century city, to release it from the accumulations of the
centuries, and to accord it the honour in Rome's monumental landscape they understood – as had Hadrian
before them – that it warranted.

In similar vein, Peter Greenaway offers the
Pantheon a profound cinematic tribute in his 1987
film *The Belly of an Architect*. It follows his protagonist
Stourley Kracklite as he mounts an exhibition in Rome
on the French enlightenment architect Étienne-Louis
Boullée, whose sublimely giant domed monument to
Isaac Newton is a tribute to Hadrian's structure. Beset
by stomach pains that recall the tale spun by Cassius
Dio that Augustus' wife Livia had brought about the
emperor's demise with poisoned figs, the architect
memorably breaks down in a blend of pain and unfettered appreciation in front of the Pantheon's portico –
Boullée demands a toast in the Pantheon's shadow,
but in the midst of a tantrum brought on by extreme
discomfort and life-threatening illness, Kracklite belts
out his applause before one of architecture's highest
achievements, ever, anywhere.

## Bathing and Everyday Life

The Pantheon was hardly the extent of Agrippa's building in the centre of the Campus Martius. The modest

suite of structures raised around the time in which the original Pantheon was built was, in the penultimate decade of the first century BC, joined by a substantial bath complex located in the block now occupied by the ecclesiastical high street of via dei Cestari, as well as gardens and an artificial lake functioning as a public pool. Its water arrived from beyond the city on the Aqua Virgo, constructed in 19 BC, and this ancient waterway would play a vital role in both the life of the ancient city and the rhetorical turn to Roman antiquity long regarded as its highly mediated rebirth, or renaissance. The remains of the Basilica of Neptune, which can be seen at the rear of the Pantheon, date to their restoration and incorporation into the once separate Baths of Agrippa (6) following the fire of AD 80, again at the instigation of Hadrian, but they offer a trace in the contemporary city of the first of the baths complexes that would play an important social role for Rome's inhabitants in the imperial era. Public bathing was a central part of Roman culture, and by the fourth-century capitulation of the Western Roman Empire more than eight hundred facilities for bathing were spread throughout the city – a number that can be broken down into various well-known types reflecting size, temperature, technology and the arrangement of their various spaces.

The Baths of Agrippa, however, belong to a category of more significant imperial structures that not only met the sanitary needs of the Romans of their day, but also extended to gymnasia and libraries, for use by men,

women and children. Built at the start of the second
century AD, the Baths of Trajan (26) are, for instance,
located near to the Colosseum, beyond Nero's Domus
Aurea, and their ruins include the impressive remains
of one of the two libraries to which patrons had access.
Massive wood-fires heated water to fill the hot baths
of the expansive *caldarium* or to make the steam that
filled the *laconicum*, a sauna of sorts. Men and women
followed different itineraries in these baths, and the use
of their different facilities cut across class and gender.
They were a place to meet and be seen, to wash, certainly, be massaged by slaves, and to attend to various
other needs of the body and the mind. Physicians were
on hand to aid those who slipped on the ornate but
slick marble or who fainted in reaction to the sudden
drop in temperature from the *caldarium* to *the frigidarium.* The *frigidarium* was ordinarily the last stop for
bathing men (it seems women were discouraged from
the extreme cold of this chamber), and the largest
example is on the opposite side of the Colosseum and
alongside via Appia Antica, the original Appian Way,
in the Baths of Caracalla (33). These baths were built
more than a century after those of Trajan, initiated by
Septimius Severus and completed by their namesake.
These, too, retain a clear imprint in Rome's landscape,
their preserved walls precisely describing the organization of their various parts.

Built at the other end of the third century AD, the
Baths of Diocletian (4, opposite Termini Station, and
thus a metro ride from Circo Massimo) easily impress

with their cavernous rooms. For those for whom the footprints and dimensions of the baths of Trajan and Caracalla alone are not enough to conjure up the atmosphere of the baths, the volumes of the Baths of Diocletian go a long way towards a remedy. They are noted here, though, for the interconnectedness of this historical and archaeological site – a concrete trace of Roman society – with the contemporary museum of epigraphs housed around the Carthusian cloisters composed by Michelangelo in the mid-sixteenth century. This museum contains thousands upon thousands of traces of everyday Roman life as recorded in commercial notices, graffiti, funerary inscriptions, public notices, and so forth, which feed a fuller image – at once closer to us and more distant from us – of the kinds of lives lived by individual Romans, and provide a counterpoint, therefore, to the abstractions that such monuments as the Baths of Diocletian themselves inevitably invite.

### 'Go Thou to Rome ...'

One of the more serene spots in Rome is in the grounds of the so-called Protestant or English Cemetery (32). John Keats and Percy Bysshe Shelley, who together lived in an apartment alongside the Spanish Steps, are both interred there, and draw many visitors through its gates. The cemetery is not exclusively, though, for either the English or the Reformed Church. There is a substantial Orthodox section; there are many

Americans, especially among the monumental graves of the nineteenth century; many foreign scholars who ended lives dedicated to the study of Rome's history, art and culture in that very city; and indeed many Italians, most notable among them being Antonio Gramsci, the father of Italian communism, and for whom a flame burns in perpetuity. (A second, military cemetery alongside the Protestant Cemetery contains Commonwealth War Graves, but trades romance for reason in its layout and atmosphere.) The southern walls of this *cimitero acattolico* are the walls, too, of the city of Rome as the Emperor Aurelian redefined them in the 270s – just one decade before Rome lost its standing as the capital of the (Western) Roman Empire to Mediolanum.

In building a new wall for Rome, Aurelian did two things. For one, he defined a new extent for the capital of the Roman Empire, recasting its edges at the height of its ancient population. For another, he captured a fleeting image of Rome, like a snapshot, before its long decline as an imperial city, and an instance, then, of a Rome that once more needed physical walls to keep its enemies at bay. Aurelian is commonly given credit for bringing to a close the turbulent period called the Crisis of the Third Century or Imperial Crisis – in which the fractures that perhaps inevitably followed a sustained period of expansion and conquest were made painfully evident at the top, and in which the capacity of the Empire to endure was not at all a given. In 235, Severus Alexander – the final link in the

Severan chain – was assassinated by his own troops, initiating a decades-long period marked by internal turmoil, claims and counter-claims to the imperium. The economy suffered; the unity of the Empire was undermined (and, consequently, Rome as its centre); and its extent diminished. Aurelian asserted Rome's military might and reunited an empire that had been divided into three largely separate parts, essentially corresponding to the Italian peninsula and Rome's territories, respectively, to its east and west. The stability he brought proved to be temporary, and not solved until the reign of Diocletian, whose twenty-year reign was truncated by his abdication in 305. His scheme of structured co-rule, with major and minor emperors in both the east and the west – the Tetrarchy – brought its own turbulence.

The Aurelian Wall extends 19 kilometres around the historical centre and contained the city's population through its peaks and troughs until the twentieth century, when the opportunities for property development on the periphery and the needs of a rapidly growing modern capital rendered it an historical artefact. The gate closest to the Protestant Cemetery is the Porta San Paolo, as it is now called, which was once the Porta Ostiense, and marks the city entrance from an arterial road that connected Rome to Ostia. The defensive towers date to the fourth-century reigns of Maxentius and the child-emperor Honorius and figure prominently in Rome's long defensive history.

The view here is dominated by a funerary monument in the form of a sizeable pyramid, in the steeper pitch of the Nubian manner, in which was interred the magistrate Caius (or Gaius) Cestius in the middle of the rule of Augustus, in the penultimate decade of the first century BC. It reminds us, first, that in Rome's most expansive phases those parts of the periphery that once lay beyond the city's extent were embraced by the fabric of the *urbs* proper – a tomb such as this would not have had a place in Augustan Rome, within, that is, the *pomerium*. It also recalls the fact that Rome was never reluctant to celebrate through imitation the most advanced of the cultures it had conquered. Caius was buried in a single-cell grave, which was sealed until the 1660s, when records on the site itself show that the tomb was explored and restored during the reign of that other great city-building *pontifex maximus*, Alexander VII. After years of contemporary restoration, the tomb is now open to the public. The remains of Caius Cestius are gone, as are most of the frescos recorded from that time, excepting a small number of vibrantly painted scholars and victories. In this sense, they are much like the city enclosed by the walls into which the pyramid is embedded. They demand an act of projection, while enough remains after the passage of two millennia that we can start to imagine how grand they might once have been.

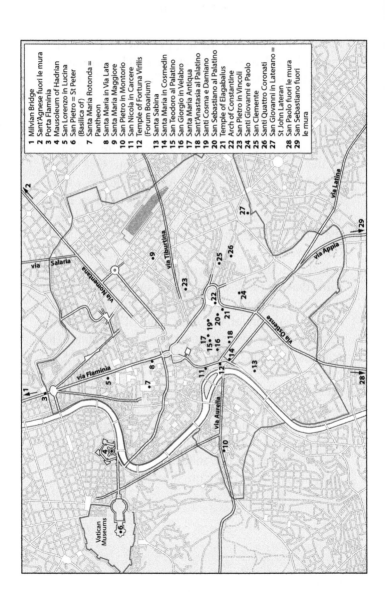

1 Milvian Bridge
2 Sant'Agnese fuori le mura
3 Porta Flaminia
4 Mausoleum of Hadrian
5 San Lorenzo in Lucina
6 San Pietro = St Peter
  (Basilica of)
7 Santa Maria Rotonda =
  Pantheon
8 Santa Maria in Via Lata
9 Santa Maria Maggiore
10 San Pietro in Montorio
11 San Nicola in Carcere
12 Temple of Fortuna Virilis
  (Forum Boarium)
13 Santa Sabina
14 Santa Maria in Cosmedin
15 San Teodoro al Palatino
16 San Giorgio in Velabro
17 Santa Maria Antiqua
18 Sant'Anastasia al Palatino
19 Santi Cosma e Damiano
20 San Sebastiano al Palatino
21 Temple of Elagabalus
22 Arch of Constantine
23 San Pietro in Vincoli
24 Santi Giovanni e Paolo
25 San Clemente
26 Santi Quattro Coronati
27 San Giovanni in Laterano =
  St John Lateran
28 San Paolo fuori le mura
29 San Sebastiano fuori
  le mura

# 3

# A Middle Age

*Saxa Rubra – Christianity under Constantine – The Basilica – A Turning Point – The Roman Church in a Christian Empire – Competing for Authority – San Clemente – The Commune of Rome*

## Saxa Rubra

Since the third century BC, via Flaminia has been the principal route north from Rome, originally setting out from the Porta Fontinalis, at the base of the Capitoline, in the Servian Wall) and closely following the path of via del Corso – what was once via Lata. With a new wall came a new gate, and via Lata ran up to the Porta Flaminia (3, now the Porta del Popolo), skewing north and east to eventually reach Ariminum (Rimini) on the Adriatic coast. Today, as you go north from the Piazza del Popolo, you are taken through a well-established twentieth-century suburb and, in the blocks extending to its east, some of the venues and the athletes' village built for the 1960 Olympic Games. This path brings you to the Tiber and to a bridge that bears the marks of more than two millennia of reinforcing, rebuilding and resurfacing to ensure safe passage or adequate defence, as needs over time have dictated. Despite the richness of the history it has witnessed, the Pons Milvius, or the Milvian Bridge (1), has long been associated with a battle staged not on the bridge per se but between this ancient landmark and the small village of Saxa Rubra a short distance further north – now swallowed up by the twentieth-century creep of the Roman periphery.

The form of rule established by Diocletian at the end of the third century was effectively a rule of four: two Augusti (principal emperors) and two Caesares (or Caesars, second-tier emperors), overseeing an empire that was split into east and west as a practical solution to the problem of ruling such a vast territory from a central capital. By and large, they ruled not from Rome, but from cities of strategic significance to the trading interests and defence of the Empire. Rome was a symbolically important city, but no longer active in the administration of the polity. From the foundation of the Tetrarchy in 293, the Augusti were Diocletian himself and Maximian, both of whom abdicated in 305, clearing the way for their respective Caesares to be elevated in the manner of heirs apparent, which they were. The death of the former Caesar Constantius in 306, and of his successor Severus (at the hands of Maxentius) the following year, provoked a power contest over the western branch of the Roman Empire. The system broke down as Constantine, the former Caesar of Gaul, Hispania and Britain and son of Constantinius, marched on Maxentius, the former Caesar of Rome.

Both Constantine and Maxentius had been elevated to the highest rank with support from different quarters. Constantine won the contest for the title of Augustus of the Roman Occidens. His rule brought about the end of the so-called Second Tetrarchy and, after a little more than a further decade's co-rule, the reinstatement of sole principality over a Roman Empire that would enjoy a brief spell of reunification – even as it witnessed the removal of imperial power from Rome as a city.

At the edge of the Forum, the enormous Basilica Nova documents the power shift that occurred at Saxa Rubra on the day, 28 October 312, when Constantine and Maxentius met in battle. Initiated by Maxentius, it was completed by the victor to an altered design. He furthermore installed a colossus in his own likeness after its completion. This is just one of the realignments to which Rome would be subject in Constantine's ascendancy. The battle of Pons Milvia is legendary, not simply because of the consequences it wrought upon the history of the Roman Empire. To the side of the path taken by via Sacra, the Arch of Constantine (22) records the victory in relief, but a more compelling account awaits the traveller who finds his or her way across the city to join the incessant throng in the papal chambers painted by Raphael, now part of the Vatican Museum. There you can join the crowd taking in the fresco (figure 3.1) on which is captured the enduring symbolism of Constantine's conquest, in a setting that owes

**Figure 3.1:** Raphael (with Giulio Romano), *Battle of the Milvian Bridge*, fresco, 1520–4. Hall of Constantine, Apostolic Palace.

everything to his victory: an early sixteenth-century rendition by Raphael and his gifted assistant Giulio Romano that celebrated the beginnings of the universal church – just as it had begun to fracture.

Constantine's newfound openness to Christianity was tempered by the greater responsibility of imperial rule. He retained the title Pontifex Maximus as a natural part of his imperium, even if he refused to enact some of the traditional religious functions of the office. His adoption of the sign of Christ was a response to what Eusebius Pamphili (in his *Life*) called a vision and what Lactantius (in his fourth-century *Constantine's Conversion*) described as a direction in a dream. Maxentius himself had been warned (writes Latantius) that he would face defeat if he left Rome, but history favours the symbolism of a Roman emperor winning in battle under the Christian sign, at Saxa Rubra and thereafter. Over the two and a half centuries since Christians had started appearing in Rome, they had endured periods of intense hostility. Constantine's vision and the success it heralded paved the way for newfound freedoms for Christians throughout the Empire just a decade after Diocletian's Great Persecution. Constantine met his eastern counterpart, Licinius, in Mediolanum to discuss the status of Christians merely four months after defeating Maxentius, in February 313. Their agreement, the Edict of Milan, resulted in the legalization of Christianity, freedom to worship and compensation for a period of systematic oppression.

Constantine's vision and the authority he drew from it paved the way for an entirely new religious basis for the rulership of the Roman Empire. The imperial court had already left Rome in the third century, and by the end of the fourth the emperor had outlawed the religions that the city had spread across the Empire – not Constantine, or not exactly, but certainly the sons and grandson who, at one point or another, succeeded him. The Curia was left in charge of a city of Romans that was, by the end of the fourth century, no longer able or willing to sustain the traditions and deities that had evolved in service of their city over nearly a millennium. That the worship of Pluto, Mithras, Venus and Jupiter would become illegal would have been unthinkable to Diocletian only a century earlier, but by the time it occurred the trajectory towards Roman Christianity was clearly enough defined.

Putting aside matters of belief, Giulio's prolific depiction of the Latin cross in his Vatican fresco is an understandable anachronism for a sixteenth-century painter, and Constantine's own labarum (military standard), depicted on various fourth-century coins and reliefs, sets the record straight. It is topped with the 'chi-rho' christogram formed from the first two letters of the Greek word for Christ – one of the oldest symbols adopted, along with the fish-shaped 'ichthys', by the Christian community. (The epigraphic museum at the Baths of Diocletian contains many early examples of its use in Rome.) The depiction of the winged Victory that heralds Constantine's win on his triumphal arch is a nod to both established and new religions in a moment of transition. This figure is unambiguously transformed and multiplied by the sixteenth century into angelic soldiers fighting for Constantine's cause. The result, however, holds: a vision that offers the promise of victory for Constantine and, through him, a faith that would become a universal institution.

## Christianity under Constantine

There is understandably much to make of this turn from an ancient, pragmatically 'pagan' Rome towards the Rome of the middle ages and the Church, caught between temporal rule and spiritual power, but we would do well to think of it as not an abrupt change so much as a tipping point. Some decades ago, the Yale historian Ramsey MacMullen observed that Constantine himself made no direct reference to Christ (or indeed any statements indicating a strong grasp of Christian theology) before 321, the year in which he decreed Sunday the Christian day of rest. Constantine's paths did not, he wrote, pass 'instantaneously from paganism to Christianity but more subtly and insensibly from the blurred edges of one, not truly itself, to the edges of the other'.[1]

In *Three Christian Capitals*, Richard Krautheimer recalls the obstacles faced by an emperor giving public legitimacy to a religion that went directly against the devotional culture that had hitherto shaped Roman life and its institutions. The Senate, which governed the city, was a bastion of the Roman aristocracy, and it would have been unthinkable to its members not to involve the gods in all aspects of their lives – especially in securing the good fortunes of the city by enacting the rites through which the gods were paid their dues. Unlike Maxentius, who had been Caesar of Rome and Augustus of Italy, Constantine was hardly a familiar face to the Romans. He visited Rome on just three occasions, favouring the imperial cities of the Baltic and expansion to the Empire's east. His gravitation towards Christianity compounded his apparent disinterest in Rome itself, causing offence among its ruling class, evidenced in his poorly received refusal on at least one occasion to make a ceremonial offering to Jupiter at his Capitoline temple as was called for by tradition. As any good ruler would, however, he rectified his missteps and enacted his role as the chief priest of the religions of Rome.[2]

Whether out of a sense of politics, tradition or devotion, Constantine demonstrated his adherence to the old religions in many ways that substantiate MacMullen's characterization of his so-called conversion. It is a notable legacy of his reign that he built for the Christian Church, and built a lot. He donated imperial lands and funds from his private purse for a building programme within greater Rome. This ended the Christians' reliance, to this point, upon the modest form of the *domus ecclesiae* – those domestic centres of worship adapted from private houses that had offered, in their anonymity, a degree of cover during periods of persecution and, in times of relative freedom, were intended neither to intrude upon nor offend the world around them. (The role of extra-mural catacombs is often recalled as a discrete setting for worship, for the celebration of the funereal feasts, or *refrigeria*, and an opportune place to hide, but these networks were neither anonymous nor exclusively used by Christians for burial.) Constantine sponsored the construction of new buildings dedicated to communal worship and the celebration of the Mass. Of the basilicae built in Rome during his reign, which are at least a dozen in number, some are opulent and others modest. Constantine's relationship with the Senate may not always have been straightforward, but by careful consideration of where to build he neutralized any reservations it might have fostered over the newfound legitimacy given to Christianity by the Edict of Milan.

The Senate had no say over what the emperor could do on his own lands within the city, and so it could not object to the raising of San Giovanni Laterano (St John Lateran, 27) or, nearby, Santa Croce in Gerusalemme. It likewise had no say on what occurred beyond the *pomerium*, and basilicae were raised *fuori le mura* (beyond the walls) in honour of, among others, St Peter (San Pietro, on the Vatican), St Paul and St Sebastian (San Paolo, 28, on via Ostiense, and San Sebastiano, 29, on via Appia), St Agnes (Sant'Agnese,

2, on via Nomentana in the city's north, alongside the family mausoleum dedicated to Santa Costanza) and St Lawrence (San Lorenzo, in the neighbourhood named for him).

You can get the sense of the remove of these sites from such centres of Roman life as the Forum or Campus Martius by walking from the Forum, past the Colosseum, to St John Lateran, which was founded by Constantine in the year of the Edict of Milan as the principal Roman basilica, its archbasilica and cathedral seat of the Bishop of Rome. (St Miltiades held that position until 314, but the great church builder St Sylvester thereafter commenced a reign that lasted until 335.) The Archbasilica of St John was built on lands confiscated from the Lateran family by Nero and which were part, therefore, of Constantine's own estate. Fitting snugly within the Aurelian Wall, the basilica towered over its otherwise sparse surrounds, but since it was beyond the view of the Forum and two or three kilometres from the Campus Martius it was, to all intents, safely out of the way. The basilica we can visit today has seen its fair share of amplifications, reflecting its unaltered status as the city's first church over more than 1,700 years. Those changes we face upon entering it were primarily conceived by Francesco Borromini in the middle of the seventeenth century, under the authority of Pope Innocent X of the Pamphili family – a restoration to its former sense of glory undermined by fire and damage during a period of fourteenth-century absence when the papacy temporarily relocated to Avignon. Even accounting for the tendency borne out in the history of church building to deprive simple structures of their modesty over time, or to enrich churches of increasingly clear traditional importance, St John Lateran knew gold from its beginnings: a personal statement of faith and support from the emperor himself, and a declaration as bold and direct as that made by the Colossus installed in his own basilica on the Forum. The Apostolic Palace (or Lateran Palace, not to be confused with the Apostolic Palace at the Vatican) was built in this same century and consecrated, like the basilica, by St Sylvester (I). It was for nearly a millennium a locus of Rome's religious administration and observance.

## The Basilica

We cannot easily accuse St Peter's Basilica of being a study in modesty. Its dome dominates the Roman skyline, and its vast interior and richly adorned surfaces much less recall the decades in which Christianity emerged from a state of illegality and began to conduct itself with the protection of imperial law than they do the end game of those protections: the Church as an empire in itself. Taking the stairs down to the Vatican Grottos, however, offers a chance to make contact with the original basilica structure – its columns shorn off to make way for the vast reconstruction envisaged by Donato Bramante at the turn of the sixteenth century, but their bases sitting as a reminder of the original, fourth-century church it came to replace – Old St Peter's – and hence of the first efforts to make way in Rome for a legitimized Christianity. The task of looking for tangible monuments from the fourth century is a little like looking for the architecture of republican Rome. In both cases, these early phases of what would come to be a great enterprise were overshadowed – sometimes early and suddenly, sometimes over centuries – by those expressions of the Church and the Empire at their greatest extent and at the height of their power. These beginnings take on, then, something of an abstract cast, but remain important nevertheless.

Constantine reigned uncontested as Augustus of the west from 313 onwards, and as Augustus of the whole Roman Empire from 324 to 337. In the space of a generation, Christianity went from being a persecuted sect to being a legalized form of worship *alongside* the pagan sects and cults, firmly on course to become the dominant religion of the Roman citizenry. The fourth century witnessed a long transition mirroring Constantine's move from one set of blurred edges to the other, from a polytheistic worldview to one formed around the Christian faith and Judeo-Christian premises. The edges of Rome's official Christianity, though, were moulded by traditions and habits shaped over many centuries. In making a departure of sorts from Roman antiquity into the millennium-long medieval epoch, the basilica was one of Rome's first and most significant religious and cultural battlegrounds.

The legalization of Christianity and the restorative donation of land and riches by Constantine had placed the Church on a path that, by the end of the fourth century, saw it transformed into the only legitimate form of worship. Rome's older religions were marginalized and then criminalized, and its gods began to fade into history. Rome entered the fourth century as the historical centre of a polytheistic empire – the largest the world had ever seen, even if its greatest extent was a thing of the past – and finished as a provincial city of increasingly symbolic value for a newly born Christian polity. It bore the very live traces of being the centre of what had become derogatively couched as a pagan world empire. The ruling families from which were drawn Rome's governing class had deep roots with the city itself and, therefore, strong ties to the gods who had smiled on the city's fortunes as it had subjugated the civilizations of the known world. Some could see the future in the entrails, as it were, and converted to Christianity; others rendered their devotion to the gods a private, indeed secret, matter.

As paganism was criminalized, all of those temples, all of those shrines, could no longer be used (openly, at least). Consider the Forum and via Sacra: its Temples of Saturn, of Roma and Venus, of Castor and Pollux; or the Temple of Jupiter, on the Capitoline. All neutralized. Since Christian worship needed to form a break from this religious past, it could not simply adapt Rome's religious architecture for its own ends. The basilica was a new kind of building in a religious sense, even though the basilica as such was a common form of secular structure, in which magistrates applied law and settled disputes and in which a populace engaged in trade and exchange. Of course, in Rome nothing was done without the blessing of the gods, and so the basilica was neutral only ever to a certain degree. But it was nonetheless a site of invention, continuity and compromise, and ultimately it came to stand as an architectural symbol for the essential modesty of Roman Christianity in its earliest incarnations.

As settings for Christian worship, basilicae quickly came to abound in Rome. The care taken by Constantine to build with discretion was no longer necessary as members of the Curia either embraced the new religion or withdrew from public view. Basilicae were sometimes placed on sites of convenience, and at other times on sites of miracles, martyrdoms or burials. From the first century AD onwards, Christians had died in Rome either for what they did or for who they were. St Paul, for instance, a Jewish Roman from Tarsus (in modern-day Turkey) who sought his right to be heard by Nero, had proselytized to the Romans and was killed on the site traditionally thought to be occupied by the aforementioned basilica of San Paolo fuori le mura (28) – St Paul beyond the Walls, on the former Ostian Way. St Paul's end is a matter of debate, although tradition dating back to the second century has him dying violently at Roman hands, perhaps beheaded. (The tomb long held to be his was excavated in 2009 and its remains were dated to the first or second century, consistent with this tradition.)

Over time, Christians came to venerate the burial places of the apostles and early martyrs, and St Peter's tomb, in particular, became inundated with visitors. Some hold Peter's death to have occurred during the bloody festivities of *dies imperii* in October AD 64, which marked a decade of Nero's rule and, after the Great Fire in July of that year, the continued pursuit of Christians, whom he declared responsible. According to an errant tradition, Peter was crucified upside-down on a spot now occupied by a beautiful *tempietto* built by Bramante at the end of the fifteenth century – part of San Pietro in Montorio (10), on the Janiculum. Constantine founded a basilica (16) on the site where St Peter had been buried (the first basilica *ad corpus*, or *ad corpo*, built over a burial), which was close to Nero's circus on the Vatican, where the official persecution of the sect resulted in its first Roman martyrs. An excavation in 1968 identified a first-century burial site believed to contain his remains, and the Baldachin of St Peter – the massive seventeenth-century canopy, designed by Gianlorenzo Bernini and supported by Solomonic columns – sits directly over that spot. From the outset, Constantine recognized the needs of this basilica, and among Rome's earliest basilicae this was by far the most sizeable, reflecting its importance to the fourth-century Christian community.

Over the next thousand years, Rome witnessed the transition of the Church from the humblest beginnings to having an imperial reach all of its own. In the Jubilee Year of 1300, Pope Boniface VIII introduced the distinction between major and minor basilicae, with the major basilicae referring to the four principal churches within the Diocese of Rome: the fourth-century basilicae of St Peter, St Paul beyond the Walls (more commonly known as San Paolo fuori le mura), St John Lateran and, built in the 430s under Pope Sixtus III, Santa Maria Maggiore (9). The Basilica of San Lorenzo fuori le mura joins these four as one of the five papal basilicae in Rome. St Peter's Basilica was significantly amplified in the sixteenth and seventeenth centuries and the Leonine City developed as the Vatican was cemented as the world headquarters of the Roman Catholic Church. The Basilica of San Paolo fuori le mura was almost entirely destroyed by fire in 1823, prompting one of the first and most complex discussions of the modern age around the matter of architectural heritage and restoration. As noted above, St John Lateran fell into disrepair during the Avignon papacy, requiring major building works, during which it was likewise enlarged and enriched. All of these papal basilicae now enjoy the baroque gloss of the recalibration of major sites of Christian worship in the Counter-Reformation, to which we will turn soon enough.

The buildings realized under Constantine's authority were not consistent in organization, size or purpose.

Some churches met the administrative and ceremonial needs of a religion that had long needed to simply make do. Some churches responded, as the Basilica of St Peter had done, to the need to venerate those who had been martyred for their faith. Others, like the Constantinian Church of the Holy Sepulchre in Jerusalem or the Church of the Nativity in Bethlehem, served as shrines for key sites of the Christian faith. Some buildings were straightforward arrangements of atrium (outside), narthex (transitional), nave (interior), altar and apse, reflecting the Roman precedent. Others were, like Santa Costanza, centralized and circular buildings, which again drew from the vocabulary of temples like that of the Temple of Vesta in the Forum, or mausoleums like that of Augustus. The more important basilicae introduced a transept, which in its later exaggeration (in the cathedrals of the middle ages) made the plan look like a Latin cross. It was a building form governed not by strict legislation but by what were once the very simple needs of the Church and its communion and, for its builders, by opportunity and reinvention.

### A Turning Point

St Paul was among the first to bring the Church to Rome. The circumstances under which St Peter died ensured that when it did flourish, it did so there. Constantine gave it credence and physical presence. After the reign of Constantine, though, Rome and its Church entered a period of marked uncertainty. From early in the fifth century, well-organized tribes from the north who had learned a thing or two from the Romans began making incursions into Italy, with Rome as a symbolic prize. The Visigoth king Alaric I put Rome to siege on three occasions between 408 and 410, each time resulting in significant gains and eventually securing access to the city and its treasures. Gaiseric the Vandal did some damage to the city when he entered with his troops in 455, and nearly a century later, in 546, the Gothic king Totila entered the city after weakening it by starvation for a year. In the meantime, in the imperial capital of Ravenna, the last of the Western Roman Emperors, Romulus Augustulus, abdicated to Odoacer in 476. Rome was no longer the centre of anywhere. It had been taken for the Gothic Kingdom and Ostrogoth Kingdom and remained a Gothic possession until the Eastern Roman Emperor Justinian sought to reclaim the most important cities of the Western Roman Empire, like Ravenna and Rome, for Constantinople in the two-decades-long Gothic War (535–54), which left no clear winner. Rome was returned, ultimately, to Constantinople as a Byzantine island in a peninsula increasingly under the control of what would become the Germanic Kingdom of the Lombards.

Gregorius Anicius was little more than a boy when the Gothic War ended, but as Gregory I, styled Gregory the Great – later St Gregory – he would do much to ensure Rome's eventual return to power through his systematization of the Church across Europe. In many respects, Gregory had an impact upon the medieval course of the Church as definitive as that of Paul in the first century. A Roman aristocrat by birth (of the Anicii family), former prefect of the city, a diplomat, skilled administrator and descendant of the fifth-century Pope Felix III (himself from a senatorial family), Gregory had entered a monastic life, but returned from it to take his place on St Peter's throne. He became Bishop of Rome in 590, a little more than a century after the Western Roman Empire had fallen to Odoacer. The centuries between the pontificates of Sylvester and Gregory had seen papal authority much diminished. The Gothic War had severely depleted the wealth of the Eastern Roman Empire and left Rome as a mere vestige of its former self and little more than a regional city at some distance from the centre of European power.

As the hold of the Roman Empire had weakened into the fifth century, and with it, the regularity of central or coordinated rule, the spread of Christianity across Europe had acquired a cellular character. It had initially followed the path of the Roman Empire, remaining where it landed as the Empire itself began to shrink, and developing customs and characteristics that differed between, say, Northumbria and Sicily. By insisting upon a shared faith, common practices and administrative regularity, Gregory drew attention back to Rome as the impoverished but central seat of the Church, instigating arrangements that went far towards predicating the Roman Curia as a religious institution. In Rome, especially, he rallied his logistical acumen behind the task of feeding a city that had more or less been left by Constantinople to its own devices, and in so doing activated the economic conditions that would give the Church temporal power in the coming centuries as it acquired lands and bound the distribution of food to the provision of spiritual nourishment.

It would be an exaggeration to say that nothing worked at this time. There were baths; and aqueducts, albeit in private hands, still supplied water to the city. It would, however, be fair to say that those without means – including the large community of those who had sought refuge in Rome from the Lombards (or Longobards) – were not living in a state of great comfort.

The power of Rome to unite the Western Empire had diminished accordingly, so that the organization of the Church followed the lines of the various kingdoms and tribal alliances of which sixth-century Europe was comprised: Franks, Ostrogoths, Saxons, Visigoths, Britani, and so forth. In the face of all this, the Basilica of Santi Cosma e Damiano (19) on the Forum stands as a reminder not to paint with too broad a brush. Incorporating part of the fourth-century Temple of Romulus, as well as the offices of the city prefect, the building was donated by Theodoric and his daughter, Amalasuntha, in 527 and dedicated to the twin martyrs – Sts Cosmas and Damian – for whom it is named. The history of these decades is not (necessarily) a chronicle of conflicts between Christians and pagans. The Empire had been officially Christian since the fourth century and had promoted conversion among all those whose lands were conquered. As Rome's borders receded, its exterior was populated by those who had set aside their own religious traditions in favour of the Roman Church (or instead, as in the Germanic uptake of Arianism, an amalgam of the old and the new), even as they no longer recognized Roman rule. Those who came to occupy the city of Rome were not necessarily pagans, then, even if their aggression towards Constantinople had them cast as such.

Celebrated for his practical sense, Gregory enacted a series of reforms that determined the place of Rome in the world across the following millennium. On the streets, he initiated a Church-led welfare programme and negotiated a rolling peace with the Lombards, who would otherwise pose a threat to the Church landholdings that quickly expanded throughout southern Italy, Sardinia and Sicily – and on which that programme relied. He built up the administrative structures of the Church to monitor spending and the flow of foodstuffs. Those charged with managing the practicalities of income and expenditure, importation and consumption, were accountable to a centralized organization.

Although they have all been overbuilt to varying degrees, a number of churches offer a material trace of this programme across several centuries: San Giorgio in Velabro (16); San Teodoro (15) at the base of the Palatine; Santa Maria in Cosmedin (14) on the Forum Boarium (made famous by the Bocca della Verità at its entrance); the fifth-century Santa Maria Antiqua in the Forum itself (17); and a short walk north, Santa Maria in via Lata (8, on the Corso) – all within a very short distance from one another, speaking to the concentration of people living in that neighbourhood, and the earliest, like San Teodoro and Santa Maria in via Lata, appropriating the older Roman stores on which the welfare centres, or *diaconae*, relied. The port area around the Forum Boarium was during these years a centre of importation and distribution, as it had been in centuries past. The sixth- and seventh-century reinvigoration of the city between the Forum and the Tiber also owes something to this process of adjusting for the needs of Christendom and a Christian Rome at its centre, reviving an area that had been all but abandoned as the public administration had atrophied and Rome's temples were left empty.

In the realm of faith, Gregory aimed at popularization by embracing not the highbrow legacy of Rome's classical age, which had in any case been thoroughly intermingled with Christian practices – the image of Rome, that is, and all it could be made to stand for – but a 'simple faith', as Krautheimer has put it, involving 'new forms of religiosity shot through with irrational and magical elements'.[3] It might be for the priests of the old order to maintain and placate a pantheon of gods; magical trees and rocks may have

been the domain of the pagan primitives of the north;
but saints and relics could work miracles.

This kind of Christianity particularly appealed
to those northern European peoples who had been
caught up in the wave of conversions emanating from
the Constantinian reforms of the fourth century but
who, through Rome's own subsequent impotence,
had melded its premises with all manner of local institutions and customs. As Krautheimer notes, '[I]t was
through [Gregory] that Rome became the missionary
center of Western and Central Europe, the organiza-
tional pivot of the Western Church, the spiritual guide
of the converted Germanic tribe, and thus both the
capital of Western Christianity and an increasingly
powerful influence in Western politics throughout
the middle ages.'[4] (The infamous proliferation of and
trade in relics owes something to this. Gregory himself, reflecting Roman values, looked with disfavour
on interference with the corpses and burial sites of the
martyrs. Others, though, sought a direct connection
with the Roman martyrs, or with the Roman practice
of venerating martyrs who might have died closer to
home.) The effects of these two achievements – restoring the centrality of the Church in Roman life, and
Rome to the centre of the Church – ran deep into the
foundations of Rome's longevity beyond antiquity. On
one hand, as a functioning (if struggling) city, Rome
was managed with great economy. The inhabited city
contracted to an area within the walls known as the
*abitato*, and parts of the *disabitato* (the emptied lands

within the Aurelian Wall) were turned over to agriculture, viticulture, ruins and small intra-mural villages. As the Church assumed control of increasingly large parts of the city, its good management of the food supply lent temporal power to a spiritual and social project.

Rome had enjoyed a period of building under the reign of Constantine – and during the papacy of Sylvester and his successors – and while the Empire protected the city, it had continued to support new buildings for the Church as well as to shore up damaged defence works, roads, bridges, and the like. Santa Maria Maggiore (9) was raised in the interval between the visit paid to Rome by Alaric and that of Gaiseric, and remains one of the few architectural documents of that moment, with its central nave and mosaics dating to the papal reign of Sixtus III in the 430s. There were many, many empty temples that might have absorbed the needs of the Church as places of worship and the administration of social services, but it was generally disinclined towards converting pagan structures for its needs. That said, a law passed in 459 allowed for the recycling of building materials from disused temples and public buildings that had fallen into such a state of disrepair that they were arguably irredeemable. We now call this process spoliation, although what 'disrepair' and 'irredeemable' might mean in any given situation appears to have been an open question. The Basilica of St Peter benefited from this provision, as did St

John Lateran, and almost any 'new' building project in Rome from the sixth century onwards. The restoration initiated in 461 by Pope Hilarius I of the fourth-century Basilica of Sant'Anastasia (18) at the base of the Palatine may have been an early beneficiary of this legal provision. But the buildings and monuments of Rome's ancient fabric would continue to be a source of construction materials until the last great ecclesiastical building boom of the seventeenth century. Put simply, the modern state of Rome's ruins owes more to sustainable building than to invasions from the north.

The first pre-Christian temple to be used as a church may not have been a temple at all, at least not in the strictest sense. Pope Boniface IV was given permission by the (Byzantine) Emperor Phocas to dedicate the Pantheon to St Mary and the Martyrs in 609 as Santa Maria Rotonda (7). The Pantheon stood alone for more than two centuries before another temple was pressed into use for the Church: Fortuna Virilis (12) on the Forum Boarium, dedicated in 872 to St Mary of Egypt. Although they had been consecrated in their own way, the redundant public buildings of Rome's imperial rule were less problematic as subjects of conversion. As the civic welfare programme expanded, demanding food stores and distribution centres, an increased number of these were converted for the needs of a sparsely populated city now concentrated on the banks of the Tiber either side of the island between Trastevere and the Capitoline hill.

## *The Roman Church in a Christian Empire*

The new kind of temporal kingdom that Rome built under Gregory and his successors grew through the action of missionaries rather than armies. It was organized centrally through an administrative regularity that harked back to a kind of Roman pragmatism that had helped to run an empire. A distant outpost of the Eastern Roman Empire, Rome was made more stable as a city. As a site of pilgrimage, it grew an economic base. Visitors came from across Europe, which fed demand for churches, accommodation, food and stables – a situation that has not changed markedly from that time to this. The earliest tourist guides to Rome were in circulation by the middle of the seventh century, and visitors reflected the geography of the Roman Empire at its most expansive. With Rome as the centre of the Church in a practical as well as symbolic sense, visitors to the city provided it with a religious constituency through which it projected a temporal authority. The sculpture placed on top of the Mausoleum of Hadrian (4) in 1753 by Flemish artist Peter Anton von Verschaffelt captures this intersection of spiritual mandate and temporal power.

In a vision ascribed to Gregory on the event of his papal ascension in 590 (or, perhaps, to his successor Boniface, as some accounts allow), the Archangel Michael alights on the monumental Mausoleum, repealing through divine interference the aggressions of flood (589), plague and Goth (590). In being assigned the name Castel Sant'Angelo, this monument reflects a turning point for the Church in the sixth century and, with it, Rome's fortunes. It stands on the banks of the Tiber overlooking the ancient Pons Aelius (Aelian Bridge, now the Ponte San'Angelo) as an imposing and powerful symbol of Rome and the Church as dual strongholds. The changes to both that Gregory put in train secured the ascendancy of the Church over a city that found no real authority in its antiquity and was beset from all sides.

Cutting forward to the dawn of the ninth century: Charles the Great (Charlemagne) was crowned Emperor of Rome by Pope Leo III on Christmas Day of the year 800. This event was a culmination of two centuries of adjustments and trades shaping Europe's landscape, feeding wars, drawing and redrawing the borders of kingdoms and duchies, and, within it all, consolidating the identification between Rome, the Church and the structures it maintained. It is no exaggeration to say that these relationships, even (or especially) in their mobility, shaped the history of Europe for a thousand years. The Frankish kings had consolidated power over western and central Europe over many decades. Charlemagne's father, Pepin the Short, had received his education at St Denis in Paris, and became King of Francia with the blessing of Pope Zachary. Pepin and Charlemagne expanded their temporal power with ecclesiastical authority, and by force, as they converted heathens to the Christian faith. Making Christians was the same as making subjects. Charlemagne inherited the crown of Francia from his father in 774, acquiring, too, the Kingdom of the Lombards, and with it much of the Italian peninsula. He maintained a special relationship with Rome, protecting its interests as his authority cast a shadow across it. Did the Church serve the holy ambitions of the Kingdom of the Franks? Or did its temporal power emanate from its religious authority, and hence Rome and the legacy of St Peter?

Pope Leo's long-lived predecessor Adrian (I) recognized Rome's position as a city under the authority of the Roman Empire in the east, as well as its continued exposure to the threat of the Lombard Kingdom, by which it was all but surrounded. A much closer ally against the Lombards than the court at Constantinople, the Franks were Christian and they offered Rome protection, eventually absorbing the Lombard crown and neutralizing the threat of further warfare. The immediacy of their presence eclipsed, though, the authority of Constantinople. Leo's election on the day of Adrian's death in 795 reflected a concern that Charlemagne might have intervened in the selection of a successor. As it happened, the Lombard king was generous to the new pope, offering land and riches, but Leo was unpopular and taken captive by a band of Romans in April 799, en route from the Lateran to San Lorenzo, who accused him of misconduct both ethical and moral. Escaping his captors, Leo sought the assistance of Charlemagne that he might return to his proper place in Rome. A period of more than a year followed in which the king considered whether he could determine a pope's innocence or guilt. He took Leo back to Rome, where a council of the Church met and determined that Leo could proclaim his innocence of the charges. His innocence accepted, his accusers were expelled from the city, and Leo was reinstated as pontiff. This all happened over the course of three weeks.

Two days after all was resolved, Leo rewarded Charlemagne's loyalty with an imperial crown – in the Basilica of St Peter, above the remains of Peter himself. This had a couple of effects on Rome's status in the centuries to come. For one, it introduced a structural ambiguity that would pursue Rome and the Church across the medieval age: did Leo (like a servant) place on Charlemagne's head a crown that was naturally his, or did Leo *crown* him, bestowing as pontiff the mantle of emperor upon Charlemagne? The *Liber Pontificalis* tells it one way, while the royal chronicles tell it the other.[5] Furthermore, in assuming the title of Roman emperor (Imperator Augustus Romanum), Charlemagne was at once claiming the mantle more recently held by the deposed Byzantine emperor Constantine VI and calling an end to the power of Constantinople over Rome. It would be another five hundred years before the term Holy Roman Empire came to describe the entity that was given form at the hands (or through the agency) of Leo, but Charlemagne quickly accepted and exercised his imperium as the head of the Frankish Empire. The various positions either left to Rome as a matter of course or available for Rome to fight for very much shaped the events that occurred at this moment, when Empire, Church and city were brought together in a single, contestable gesture.

At the heart of matters, however, is the authority that was acquired by Rome and its later emperors in the early desecration of the Church. The Carolingian hymn *Felix per omnes festum mundi cardines* contains, in its seventh stanza, this proclamation:

> O happy Rome, stained purple
> with the precious blood of so many princes!
> You excel all the beauty of the world,
> not by your own glory, but by the merits
> of the saints whose throats you cut with bloody
>     swords.[6]

Rome may have had a claim to a past of such legendary stature that Charlemagne's new imperium would be a fitting extension of his monarchy over the Frankish and Lombard domains. Its currency, however, rested not upon the deeds of Augustus and Hadrian, but on the martyrdom (or purported martyrdom) of the early Christians.

Some of the most holy sites in Christianity were in Rome, and when the relic trade failed to satisfy those who found their faith renewed through proximity to the saints and martyrs, there was still the option of undertaking a dangerous and arduous voyage to visit the city itself. From the sixth century onwards, Rome welcomed pilgrims and their purses. In this historical landscape, Sts Peter and Paul had long stood out above all others, but they kept a large and diverse company. The so-called Salzburg Itinerary, *Notitia ecclesiarum Urbis Romae*, systematically took pilgrims around 106 cemeteries, churches and other holy sites, inside and beyond the Aurelian Wall. Each of the major roads in and out of Rome passed by cemeteries, martyriums and basilicae *ad corpus*: via Aurelia, via Flaminia, via Salaria (old and new), via Ostiense, via Nomentana, via Tiburtina, via Latina and, of course, via Appia. And within the walls, sites of various kinds line the incursion of arterial roads into the medieval city centre, thus shaping the pattern of the *abitato*.

This guide was amplified over time, but its original core dated to the mid-seventh-century papacy of Honorius I – a pope later anathematized for his theology, but who did much to raise and restore basilicae above the graves of the Roman martyrs. The Constantinian Basilica of Sant'Agnese fuori le mura (2) was restored under his authority and with great opulence, something documented, not least, in the Byzantine depiction of Honorius standing alongside the saint, holding a model of the basilica itself.[7] Many churches that had been built under Constantine or in the immediate wake of his reign and which had fallen into disrepair across the fifth and sixth centuries received, like Sant'Agnese, a new lease on life into the eighth and ninth centuries – an act reflecting Rome's stronger position in the world, but also recognizing the

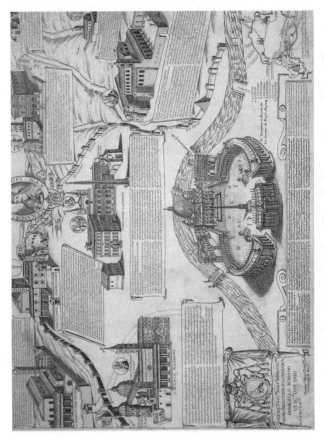

**Figure 3.2:** Map of the Seven Pilgrim Churches of Rome by Giacomo Lauro and Antonio Tempestra, ca. 1600.

close relationship between grandeur and status in the practice (and economy) of pilgrimage. This is reflected in the Einsiedeln Itinerary (figure 3.2), likely dating to before the middle of the ninth century. Leading visitors and Romans alike through cross-sections of the ancient and medieval city, it offered an experience of Rome's holy sites in the broader and deeper setting of its ancient artefacts.[8]

Gregory the Great had reinvented the administration of the Church, and in doing so had given Rome a new position within Italy and the tattered ruins of the Western Roman Empire as the wellspring of Christendom. The martyrs gave Rome symbolic importance and compelled its allies to offer it protection. Its position at the centre of a vast ecclesiastical system combined with the immediacy of objects of veneration fed a sustained programme of building *ex novo*, restoration and adaptation. And it defined a contesting set of principles that gave rise to a steady flow of conflicts and compromises between the Church, the major Roman families and the new Roman Empire of Western Europe: all of which understood Rome as properly theirs.

## Competing for Authority

The equestrian statue of Marcus Aurelius in the Campidoglio is a replica, its original sitting protected nearby in the Capitoline Museums. The original was moved to the Capitoline from its long-standing spot outside the Lateran Palace (alongside 27) by Michelangelo, architect of the Campidoglio, under the instructions of the Farnese pope Paul III. Although its survival through the middle ages is sometimes credited to a misidentification of the figure of Marcus Aurelius as Constantine, the statue has long been a magnet for expressions of dissent. (Think of Domenico's speech in Tarkovsky's 1983 film *Nostalghia*.) And for punishment.

In 964, Otto the Great, whom some name as the first of the Holy Roman Emperors, had sought to depose Pope John XII to answer a number of charges for conduct that history would seem to support as being full of irregularities, both canonical and moral. It is worth noting that the young pope, 25 or less at the time of his election, had crowned Otto two years earlier and founded as an archbishopric the imperial Saxon city of Magdeburg. Perhaps relevant, too, is that John was of the House of Tusculum, from whom the Colonna descend, and son of the Roman ruler Alberic, whose deathbed wish was to see him named pontiff. Alberic resented being ruled by those Rome had, as an Empire, itself once ruled. Otto deposed John soon after his coronation as emperor and installed an antipope of his choosing: Leo VIII. Although Leo was Roman, he did not have the support of the citizenry, who rejected Otto's authority to intervene and demanded John's return. John denounced Leo and Otto and anyone of authority who might call him to heel, since no earthly soul had authority over the pope. He died before Otto could call him fully to account. (There are some colourful speculations as to what exactly he was up to as he drew his last breath.) From Otto's point of view, this restored Leo as the rightful pope. From the perspective of the Romans, it cleared the way for a new election, which placed Benedict V on the Throne of St Peter. Like Leo, Benedict was a Roman. Unlike Leo, he was not in the implied vassalage of the emperor, but Benedict's papacy lasted merely a month and a day. Otto marched upon and besieged Rome; the Romans capitulated, and Leo was restored. His papacy ended as it was meant to just nine months later, at which point the whole thing kicked off once more – variations upon a theme.

On the death of Leo VIII, the Roman families sought the reinstatement of their own candidate, Benedict, who died before the matter could be resolved. John XIII (John of Narni) was a compromise: he was appointed by Otto, endorsed by Rome and a member of the aristocratic family of the Crescentii. But upon his appointment he set about to shore up imperial author-ity against that of the city fathers, who were having none of it, and who expelled him from Rome. Otto had appointed one Pietro (or Peter) as the city prefect, but Pietro sided with the disaffected Romans over his emperor. Otto came to set matters right, entering the city in 966, whereupon a dozen *decarones* (senior city officials) were hanged for the action – as was Pietro, for an unspecified period of time, by his hair, from the statue of Marcus Aurelius, before being flogged and paraded through the city seated backwards on an ass, then consigned to prison and finally exiled.

It neither starts nor ends there, but the imagery of Pietro, strung up by Otto at the Lateran Palace, is a telling document of the unclear position occupied by Rome in the world at this time. The Church held itself to be above the Crown, bestowing upon the emperor his imperium. The emperor held all in his domain to be his subjects, including the officers of Christendom, who lent so much structure to the Frankish Empire. Many Romans thought themselves above it all: the Church was Rome's gift to the world; so too the Empire, which was a Roman Empire after all, not simply modelled on the empire founded by Augustus, but its inheritance. Like the living subject of an unauthorized biography, the reality of Rome agitated the image on which the Empire maintained its symbolic authority, just as the Church's recent arrival in the city, relatively speaking, with the persons of St Peter and St Paul, was a sticking point among those who understood their positions in the Roman social structure to reach back to Diocletian and beyond.

From the days of Charlemagne, the new Roman emperors had resided, when they came to Rome at all, at either the Apostolic Palace at the Vatican or the Lateran Palace – two of the most significant sites of papal power across the middle ages. The German emperors did not have their own palace in Rome, which was as much a matter of practicality as it was an admission that Rome's rhetorical importance to the

Empire did not match its geo-political or institutional significance. After many years of relative inattention to Rome, Otto III reinvigorated an imperial enthusiasm for the city amidst adolescent ambitions to clothe it in gold and raise it up as the true centre of the Holy Roman Empire. It was a naïve goal reflecting his inexperience – he had received the German crown at the age of 3, but did not get to use it before he turned 16, and at the end of his regency he went straight for Rome to be crowned emperor in 996. He initiated work on an imperial palace, which was long held to have been on the Aventine, although scholars have recently come to favour the more obvious possibility that he had sought to build on the Palatine, specifically among the ruins of the Domus Augusti in proximity to the church now called San Sebastiano al Palatino (20). (This church was rebuilt among the Palatine vineyards of the Barberini family in the seventeenth century, alongside the ruined third-century Temple of Elagabalus – 21.)

As it happens, Otto's ambitions were curtailed. Obliged to leave Rome to attend to another of his cities, he felt the sting of Roman rebellion and never returned. His short-lived reign was ended by illness in 1002 and Rome's eleventh century evolved into something less like a return to imperial glory than a long negotiation of its own stake in the imperial project. Although the ninth century had given Rome a new currency in the European scheme of things, the fact that anything in these years was built at all seems a minor miracle. Families fought other families for and against the pope; the city was divided into competing strongholds, in which streets and bridges were impermeable to the enemies of those who barred access. Familial factions were with the emperor, against the pope, or with the pope, against the emperor, and the contest for authority over papal succession was subject to waves of violent destruction – all of which was exacerbated by the invasion of Rome by the forces of the Norman king Robert Guiscard in 1084. The campanile towers adorning many churches and civic structures at this time were not necessarily intended as watchtowers, but they were doubtless put to use as such. (The twelfth-century reconstruction of both Santa Maria in Trastevere and Santa Maria in Cosmedin are good extant instances of these towers.) Foreign forces were inevitably supported by one or other Roman faction fighting for the strategic upper hand on any number of bases. The authority of the Church and the promise of a truly Christian city had, for instance, lent an authority to some Roman families; others relied on the authority garnered from the immediacy of the evidence of Rome's antiquity and the position it implied against the Church and either for or against the Empire. No one position was immutable, and the history of these centuries abounds with instances of partisan mobility among Rome's established families.

The eleventh- and twelfth-century city was filled with those same monuments and markers that had brought the seventh-century pilgrims through its gates.

It was filled, too, with the remnants of antiquity: all the monuments we can see today and all those others not yet vandalized to realize the building booms of the fifteenth, sixteenth and seventeenth centuries.[9] When the canon Benedict wrote his guide to the marvels of Rome (*Mirabilia Urbis Romae*) in the 1140s, his attention was drawn not to sites of Christian importance but to the ancient world of Rome at the centre of an empire. It was not a casual antiquarianism so much as a politically infused invocation of Rome's best days and of the structures of governance that secured them for its citizens: a time of consuls and senators, able to put down those enemies who would breach its walls. It called on visitors to regard this grand past at a crucial moment: when the Church was in the ascendancy, and when the leading Roman families required a strong sense of Rome itself in order to grasp the reins of power within a city at the centre of the world. The 1140s would witness an effort to restore the city to its people through the foundation of the Commune of Rome, to which we will turn shortly.

## San Clemente

Rome's path through the thousand years of change initiated by Constantine's victory over Maxentius is not straightforward; it is complicated by ceaseless negotiations over the true legacy of the Roman Empire and the true nature of its enduring authority over the institutions of the medieval present; it is marked by fundamental transitions in worldview, sweeping rearrangements of the city's organization, constantly shifting political and military alliances, and, throughout it all, Rome's position in Christendom. As a city, much of Rome was returned to nature (and the ruin) and agriculture – what in the sixteenth century would be called the *disabitato*, the uninhabited land within the Aurelian Wall. By the eighth century, its absolute nadir, there were perhaps only three or four people left in the city for every hundred who had lived there in the time of Augustus. And in those built-up areas that remained inhabited, history piled up further: medieval accretions added to monuments of antiquity; temples, warehouses and other buildings from an era safeguarded by Roman gods adapted to the needs of the Church; marble and granite stripped from one building to realize another; towers built, towers destroyed; homes built, homes destroyed; Romans fighting Lombards, Franks, Germans, Normans, Saracens and each other; kingdom versus kingdom on Rome's behalf; the Church against the city; the Church against the Empire; the Church against itself; the city against the Empire. This rich history adds up to a ceaseless contest between competing images of Rome as a city in (and above) the world, competing bases for its authority and competing legacies, therefore drawing on the lines reaching out from the past and leading towards the future. Every one of these contests was played out through the fabric of the city.

Sitting in an outlying part of the *abitato*, the Basilica

of San Clemente offers a stratified cross-section of this problem that speaks to the slow and steady emersion from antiquity towards the powerful position from which Rome ruled the Christian world in the thirteenth century. Located today on via Labicana between the Colosseum and the Lateran, the Basilica stands as a testament to the triumphant rise of the office of the papacy over that of all other institutions – a moment of clarity emerging from a morass of ambiguities and discordance spanning the ninth to the eleventh centuries. Pope Gregory VII is credited with forcing the issue of papal sovereignty in his conflicts with the Emperor Henry IV. Gregory excommunicated Henry on three occasions; Henry facilitated the removal of Gregory and the installation of an antipope, Clement III (Guibert of Ravenna), having taken Rome in 1083 (a third attempt to assert his control over the city). Gregory held the Castel Sant'Angelo and his allies the Corsi and Pierleoni family held the Capitoline and Tiber Island, respectively, for a time at least. (The tower standing guard over the Ponte Cestio is a document of the Pierleoni occupation of the Island, as is the incongruous house standing opposite San Nicola in Carcere (11) at the intersection of Vico Jugario and via del Teatro Marcello) Gregory sought the assistance of the Norman Robert Guiscard, whose 'Sack' of 1084 brought to a head, and in the pope's favour, the conflict between Gregory and Henry.[10] Guiscard's soldiers were destructive even as he liberated Gregory, and Rome turned against them both. Gregory died in exile, but not before having defended a principle of papal supremacy – Rome as the seat of the Church over the Holy Roman Empire – that would find its most expansive fulfilment just over a century later with the pontificate of Innocent III.

Among the damage done by Guiscard was the destruction of the fourth-century Basilica of San Clemente (25), dedicated to the first-century Pope Clement I, an early successor to St Peter. The original church was erected in the upsurge of church building that followed Constantine's religious reforms, as were the nearby Santi Giovanni e Paolo (24), San Lorenzo in Lucina (5) in the Campo Marzio, Santa Sabina (13) on the Aventine and San Pietro in Vincoli (23, with Michelangelo's 'horned' depiction of Moses). San Clemente shares a common history for being restored in the Carolingian era. As Ranierius, the future Pope Paschal II had served as its cardinal priest at the time of its destruction by Norman soldiers, and witnessed them ravaging with fire the nearby monastery and church of Santi Quattro Coronati (26), likewise dating to either the fourth or fifth century. Paschal oversaw the reconstruction of both buildings – a scaled-down and reorganized version of Santi Quattro Coronati, still a veritable fortress; and a lavish new church for San Clemente, superimposed on its fourth-century foundations, although several metres above the datum of the original. The atriums (or atria) in each complex pay tribute to the Roman architecture of the fourth and fifth centuries, broadly speaking in the context of a wider appreciation of the model of ancient Rome as it had been celebrated in Benedict's *Mirabilia* – and thus paying tribute to an earlier, formative moment in the history of the Church at a time when it was once more asserting its place in the world.

San Clemente (figure 3.3) builds upon Rome's history symbolically, therefore, but also literally. Its twelfth-century reconstruction under Paschal sits almost directly upon the slightly larger footprint of the fourth-century basilica, which began life above ground but was below street level, or almost, by the twelfth century. Indeed, it proved necessary to the church builders of the twelfth century to slice off the top part of the walls to raise the new structure, and the supports of the upper basilica penetrate down through the older church – which was unused, and then unknown, from the time of reconstruction to the middle of the nineteenth century. Stairs now lead down to the narthex of the earlier structure, and further, in turn, to the structure on which the basilica itself was built. For under the church are the well-preserved and sprawling remains of a first-century AD (pre-Christian) house that had belonged to someone of means and stature, which included a warehouse and (later) a domestic altar to Mithras. The house had at some point in the first century functioned as a *domus ecclesia*, but not continuously, as the second-century Mithraeum bears out. It is possible that this, too, may all have been raised on the ashes of a house of republican-era

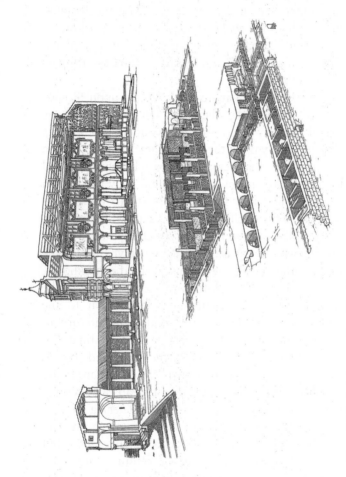

**Figure 3.3:** Exploded perspective of San Clemente.

origins that was destroyed by the Great Fire of AD 64. The ornate interior we can visit today is an eighteenth-century restoration of Paschal's reconstruction, but the stunning mosaics remain a vivid record of its medieval worldview. Just as the frescos in the lower church recall that earlier chapter in the life of the basilica, lower still, the surviving Mithraeum reminds us of the world of compromises to which these transitions were inevitably subject.

No cross-section in Rome compares with this for its legibility and significance. In San Clemente, we discover the Roman foundations of a structure that, in the twelfth century, invoked Rome's authority over Christendom. Its authority was theological, of course, and fulfilled, in a way, with the Lateran Council of 1215, which proclaimed papal primacy and confirmed Frederick II as Holy Roman Emperor – the last thorn in the side of the papacy before the reign of his successor, Conrad of Swabia, concluded the Hohenstaufen dynasty and weakened, with its end, the authority of the Empire over Rome. While the thirteenth century confirmed Rome's pre-eminence among cities, as *caput mundi*, chief city in a religious empire, it was undermined as the turn of the fourteenth century heralded a crisis of Rome's identification with the Church and with it the basis for its position in the world of Christendom.

## The Commune of Rome

The twelfth-century reconstruction of San Clemente and Santi Quattro Coronati could be misinterpreted as heralding a long-overdue peace. The balance of power in Rome – between the influential families, religious factions and the Empire – was fragile and repeatedly unsettled. Krautheimer recalls that Urban II, who was elected in 1088, spent more than half of his eleven-year pontificate effectively barred from Rome. Urban was no slouch: he launched the First Crusade, and adopted the Curia as a model of ecclesiastical management. However, he was French, and hence a foreigner, and regularly required the protections of the 'fortified mansions' of the Pierleoni – even his funerary procession (1099) was rerouted to accommodate the occupation of the Ponte Sant'Angelo by supporters of Clement III (Guibert of Ravenna). It was a city riven by factions and drawn in by temporary declarations of peace. The Concordat of Worms in 1122 would seem to have offered one such moment – Callixtus II and Henry V finding agreement over the problematic investiture of bishops, upon which hinged the question of papal authority within (and therefore over) the Holy Roman Empire. But the papal election held after the death of Honorius II in 1130 started a new series of conflicts: two elections held by two colleges refusing to regard the other as legitimate; and hence the investiture of two popes, Innocent II, the creature of the German King Lothair and the

Frangipani family, and the Pierleoni Anacletus II (traditionally the antipope), who holed up in the Castel Sant'Angelo while simultaneously coordinating raids on the city's churches.[11]

Amidst all of this, the declaration in 1143 of a Roman Republic, ruled for the people by a Senate, reinstated the ancient hallmark of Roman self-governance (and self-determination) bound up in the acronym SPQR. Asserting the primacy of Rome over both the Church and the Empire, the Senate was comprised of fifty-six citizens, both noble and less so, led by a patrician (*patricius*). This was, in the first instance, another Pierleoni, Jordanus, who, although a brother of Anacletus (who died in 1138), had not supported him. The pope, Innocent II, was invited in the clearest of terms to surrender his temporal wealth and power to the Roman Republic and to focus on matters spiritual, leaving the people of Rome to take care of all his earthly concerns. Demonstrating how easy it would be to serve the Church unburdened by riches, the city ransacked a number of the *palazzi* belonging to members of the cardinalate. By way of response, Pope Lucius II (elected into this situation in 1144) used a combination of guile and brute force to end what had from the time of his election rapidly evolved from a state of insurgency into the Commune of Rome. Of course, it was not only the Church that the Senate regarded as subordinate to its authority. After a decade of equivocating with Lucius and his successors, Eugene III and Anastasius IV, and with the king of the Romans, Conrad III, by the middle of the 1150s Rome faced both a new pope and a new emperor. The Senate offered to crown the king who deigned to rule in the name of Rome, Frederick I Barbarossa (Hohenstaufen). He declined the privilege in favour of a papal coronation (by the English pope Adrian IV, in 1155), which, as Krautheimer states so succinctly, 'ended in the customary bloody battle with the Romans in the Borgo, and in the equally customary malaria epidemic, which forced a quick retreat on the part of the Germans'.[12]

The stand-off was resolved in 1188 through the intervention, ultimately, of Clement III, who within a year of his election to the papacy had figured out how to return temporal power to the pontiff and to restore the property that had been transferred from the Church to the city over the preceding half-century. A city administration emerged from the peace – a peace in which the Senate was subordinate to the pope, who chose its leader – and the ascendancy of the papacy secured authority not just over the city but also over the Empire.

Today, the mayor and councillors of Rome meet in the Palazzo Senatorio (or Palazzo del Senatore) on the Capitoline hill (figure 3.4) – a building designed by Michelangelo in the sixteenth century to over-write several other layers, structures both ancient and medieval, and completed by Giacomo della Porta in the first years of the seventeenth century. The tower was commissioned by Pope Nicholas V in the middle

**Figure 3.4:** Lucas van Doetecum (after Hieronymus Cock), *View of the Campidoglio on the Capitoline Hill, with Equestrian Statue at Lower Right* [and Palazzo Senatorio at the rear], engraving, 1562.

of the fifteenth century, and the square it faces stands as a compositional study in the anticipation of democratic process – all parts working together in harmony towards common ends (as James Ackerman suggested in his classic study on Michelangelo).[13] The site has a rich early modern history of serving this goal. It was likely here that the Senate met during the decades of communal rule, from the 1150s through to the 1180s: a structure built upon the ancient ruins of the republican Tabularium, or official records office, parts of which remain visible from the Forum. Another structure had been raised in its place from around the end of the twelfth century, and a new Palazzo del Senatore was built across the second half of the thirteenth, its towers standing proud atop of the Capitoline, but in no less need of fortifications, despite the apparent security of its position. Rome's situation, too, may have seemed deceptively inviolate. The rising importance and power of the French monarchy had come to exert a significant force upon the French papacy of Clement V, who in turn was a pawn in the high-stakes tussle over European power. The *Cathedra Petri* was moved to Avignon in 1309, thereby marking a long period of absence on the part of the Church from Rome. The city was under the now distant control of a distinctly French papacy, but otherwise left to its own devices.

The insurgency fomented in the decade spanning 1344 and 1354 by the popular leader Cola di Rienzo – self-proclaimed Tribune of Rome and would-be uniter of all Italy – speaks to the possibilities available to those Romans possessing an expansive imagination and an impatience with life on the margins. The episode is full of familiar moves: conflicts between powerful families; the Empire pitted against the Curia; the Curia against the Roman barons; and that oft-repeated belief in Rome as the sacrosanct wellspring of all power and authority. Cola did not have the force of history at his back, and he met his end, eventually, under ignominious circumstances, but his example reassures us that the departure of Clement V for the Kingdom of Arles in 1309 barely affected the continuity of Rome as Rome. And the return of the papacy and the Curia, nearly a century later, was a return, too, to the complex exchanges that had shaped Rome's middle ages. In the fifteenth century, a fresh start would imbue such exchanges with a fresh hue. And it is to this episode that we now look.

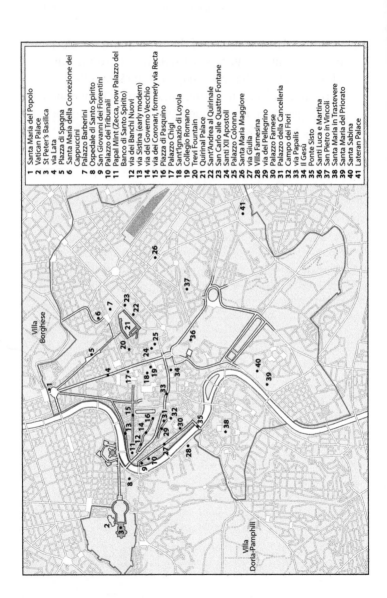

1 Santa Maria del Popolo
2 Vatican Palace
3 St Peter's Basilica
4 via Lata
5 Piazza di Spagna
6 Santa Maria della Concezione dei Cappuccini
7 Palazzo Barberini
8 Ospedale di Santo Spirito
9 San Giovanni dei Fiorentini
10 Palazzo dei Tribunali
11 Papal Mint (Zecca, now Palazzo del Banco di Santo Spirito)
12 via dei Banchi Nuovi
13 via Sistina (early modern)
14 via del Governo Vecchio
15 via dei Coronari, formerly via Recta
16 Piazza di Pasquino
17 Palazzo Chigi
18 Sant'Ignazio di Loyola
19 Collegio Romano
20 Trevi Fountain
21 Quirinal Palace
22 Sant'Andrea al Quirinale
23 San Carlo alle Quattro Fontane
24 Santi XII Apostoli
25 Palazzo Colonna
26 Santa Maria Maggiore
27 via Giulia
28 Villa Farnesina
29 via del Pellegrino
30 Palazzo Farnese
31 Palazzo della Cancelleria
32 Campo dei Fiori
33 via Papalis
34 Il Gesù
35 Ponte Sisto
36 Santi Luca e Martina
37 San Pietro in Vincoli
38 Santa Maria in Trastevere
39 Santa Maria del Priorato
40 Santa Sabina
41 Lateran Palace

**4**

# Return to Rome

*The Theatre of the World – Decades of Return – Decades of Rebirth – A Papal City – Two Projects – The Sack of 1527 – A Slow Transition – A Rhetorical Renewal – Barberini and Beyond – A Monument in the Making*

### *The Theatre of the World*

Walking into the vast public space that sits before St Peter's Basilica (3) is like stepping onto a world stage (figure 4.1). The internet-era death of Pope John Paul II in 2005, election and resignation of Benedict XVI and election in 2013 of Pope Francis, spawned a pro-liferation of startling images as the faithful from around the world flocked into this piazza. Spilling into the surrounding city, they twice awaited the first glimpse of portentous white smoke rising from the chimney of the Chapel of Sixtus IV in the Apostolic Palace. As the smoke cleared, a new Bishop of Rome appeared on the balcony of the Benediction Loggia – directly beneath the pronounced familial inscription 'Burghesius' indelibly associated with Paul V (born Camillo Borghese), who was, in many important respects, the architect of this particular spectacle. As a form of institutionalized theatre, there is nothing new in the scene of the

**Figure 4.1:** Piazza of St Peter's Basilica, by Gianlorenzo Bernini, completed 1667.

faithful gathering before the Holy Father, although, thanks to social media, its image is now infinitely more immediate and recognizable. In the mould of his predecessors Urban VIII (of the Barberini family) and Innocent X (Pamphili), the seventeenth-century Chigi pope Alexander VII effectively demonstrated that Rome as a whole could serve the Church as its arena. Alexander went so far as to stage-manage the entire city, giving the nod to an extraordinary number of projects, including his own Palazzo Chigi (17, now the official residence of the Italian Prime Minister), the regularization of the ancient via Lata (4), manipulation of the Piazza del Popolo (around his family church of Santa Maria del Popolo, 1) and the formalization of the tridentine zoning of the streets of the Campo Marzio.

No stage, however, was more expansive or overwhelming than the piazza designed by Gianlorenzo Bernini under Alexander's authority and completed in the year of the pontiff's death, 1667.

Much has been said – intelligent and otherwise – about its symbolism and effect. It is enough to recognize that it functions as a kind of rhetorical claim upon Rome's singular importance in the geography of Christendom – a position that a mere century earlier seemed far from given. From a distance it works as a monumental gesture emanating out from the basilica, both from the air, as an imprint on the city that rivals Rome's stadia both ancient and modern, and in the grand avenue extending from the Castel Sant'Angelo – the 'rationalization' of a rabbit warren of structures that had accumulated over centuries in the Borgo, one that Bernini had already envisaged, but which was not completed until after the Second World War. Enveloped by the two arms that extend out from the basilica itself, it is a machine set in motion by its inhabitants. As you walk towards the steps of St Peter's, four rows of modest Tuscan columns seem to shift in and out of alignment even as they are held in place by a simple, inscribed entablature; close to a hundred statues depicting saints of all descriptions supervise the scene – conceived but not executed by Bernini. More than this, though, the piazza is overwhelmingly large, like the interior that follows. To stand in the piazza of St Peter's Basilica is to become both an actor in the theatre of the Church and a spectator in the word's purest sense: taking in, or being prepared to take in, the spectacle of the pontiff as he addresses the world from its absolute core.

The granite obelisk in the centre connects the piazza to a history of Roman theatricality. It is surely one of the oldest artefacts anywhere in the city, and within our current century it will reach an age of four and a half millennia. It originated in Heliopolis before being moved by Augustus to Alexandria and by Caligula to the Circus of Nero, the Vatican circus over which the Piazza di San Pietro overlaps in an eternal retort to the persecutions inflicted there upon Christians. It was a mammoth and well-documented engineering feat on the part of Domenico Fontana (sixteenth-century architect to the Fabric of St Peter's) to relocate it to its prominent setting in front of the new basilica, which he did in 1586 on the instructions of Sixtus V, pre-dating the completion of the basilica by two decades. Bernini took these raw materials – obelisk, basilica and square – and brought them together into one of the most expertly choreographed experiences one can have in this city, even today.

Starting this chapter here, though, is to give away the ending of one storyline through which Rome's early modern history unfolds over the course of three centuries. At the end of the fourteenth century, the presence of the Church in Rome was sorely diminished. The *Cathedra Petri* had been moved to Avignon, and the fifteenth century would be spent in the restitution of a largely deserted city, central but now provincial, and spent, too, in carving out a position for Rome in the power landscape of the early modern European era. The construction of the Piazza of St Peter's was a crowning act of sorts recognizing that the identification of Rome with a religious empire reaching to the farthest expanse of the known world was a position that was hardly inevitable and that was far from assured as the pontiff made his way back to the city from France. When Pope Gregory XI returned to Rome in 1377 (purportedly at the behest of Catherine of Siena), it was to a city of only somewhere between ten and twenty thousand people that had been reclaimed by the Roman families for the Romans. Over time, though, and involving inevitable conflict, it would once again become a Rome for the Church and, hence, for the world.

## Decades of Return

For many decades across the thirteenth and fourteenth centuries, the walls built by Leo IV had little to protect, and both the twelfth-century Vatican Palace of Eugene III (2) and the fire-damaged Lateran Palace (41) were all but abandoned. In an extreme evocation of the trade of Rome as a living city for Rome as an abstract ideal, the physical absence of the pope from the Lateran was reconciled with the principle *ubi papa, ibi Roma*; Rome was wherever the pope happened to be – which left unresolved the question of what the city's role might be in his absence if it was not engaged with hosting the Church. Gregory XI returned the Curia to Rome, taking up residence first at the Basilica of Santa Maria in Trastevere (38) and then at Santa Maria Maggiore (26). He had broken a fast of sorts, but it was forty years before his nominal successor ended the so-called Western Schism that had opened up in the Church as a consequence of his gesture.

Born in 1328, Gregory XI had never had occasion to see Rome before his dotage. He died within a year of his arrival, in 1378, prompting a brief conclave held at the Basilica of St Peter to elect a successor. This was the first Roman conclave since the Curia decamped to Avignon, and it was stormed by a party of Rome's citizens, determined to install one of their own to St Peter's throne – a desire not only to interrupt the French lineage that had lent weight to the decision to render Avignon a Rome of sorts, but also to reinstate the insistently Roman character with which the papacy had once been properly imbued. The move to Avignon may have made a signal break from the city, but the papal palaces in Orvieto and Viterbo even today testify to a weakened connection to Rome itself before 1308. The Neapolitan Urban VI fitted the bill (just), but he was elected from outside the College of Cardinals and a French contingency declared that the forced nature of his election had in any case invalidated the result. An antipope was consequently installed in Avignon with the name Clement VII – not to be confused with the Medici pope who would reign with that name more than a century later.

The ensuing conflict within the Western Church continued on into the fifteenth century, when Gregory XII honoured a deal under which he would resign if the reigning antipope did so first, freeing up an opportunity for a fresh election in 1417 (this being the last papal renunciation before, nearly six centuries later, the resignation of Benedict XVI). Even this conclave, though, was in Rome only in spirit, since the cardinalate had gathered in Constance, the German setting for negotiation of a solution to a pointy religio-political problem and a safe distance from the possibility of Roman interests confusing Church matters.

And so in the person of Martin V (Colonna) – a name with solidly Roman credentials, but an individual who had supported the antipopes Alexander V and John XIII – the office once more returned, physically and symbolically, to Rome and St Peter's in 1420. He maintained a residence first at the Basilica of Santa Maria Maggiore, as Gregory XI had done before him, and later at the sixth-century Basilica of Santi XII Apostoli (24), the Church of the Twelve Apostles, which sits alongside his family palace, the Palazzo Colonna (25).

This Rome, then, was a city that served the world of Christendom as a hard-won inheritance. It required care and investment to once again become a thing of splendour for the Church. After the false start of Gregory XI's return, Martin definitively restored the papal office to a Rome that was ambivalent about this development – even as it might have welcomed the baser advantages of the reinstatement of the Curia to the city. Indeed, neither the principle of the pope's embodiment of Rome nor the history of fifteenth-century Rome as the history of the institution of the Church accounts particularly well for the interests of the thoroughly established families and the interests of the Senate. The fifteenth century therefore witnessed a contest in which the idea of Rome became even more mobile than it had been before this time. In earlier centuries, the pope might have, in principle, ruled the city, but in the absence of the Holy See it operated under a secular form of civic management. In the middle of the fifteenth century, the Church did not have the natural claim to rulership over Rome that it had set aside more than a hundred years earlier.

Rome was not a particularly large city at the start of the century. Its population was considerably diminished in comparison with those centuries that had seen Rome take command over Europe – either as its empire or as Christendom. Compounding the administrative evacuation to Avignon, the Black Death had left, at one estimation, a mere seventeen thousand in the city over which Cola di Rienzo had himself declared Tribune in 1347 – at best guess less than 2 per cent of the city's population at the height of the Roman Empire's reach. Nonetheless, its leading families did not easily forget that the Church had turned its back on the city while continuing to claim Rome for itself. On his death in 1431, Martin V was succeeded by the Venetian Eugene IV (Condulmer), who suffered the ignominy of a civic uprising led by the Colonna, being the family of his predecessor, who had granted them numerous favours (too numerous, said Eugene, who had promptly overturned them). The image of his escape in 1434 down the Tiber to a friendlier Florence, dressed as a Benedictine monk, his boat copping a rain of stones, is a vivid reminder of the tenuous hold the institution had over this city in these years. A peace was negotiated between the Curia and the Colonna and Eugene returned a decade after his flight, only to vacate the throne again in the usual fashion in 1447, thereby making way for Pope Nicholas V.

## Decades of Rebirth

It is tempting to see a new era of *renascence* arrive with the pontificate of Nicholas. That would be, though, to ignore the slow and unsteady negotiation of the papacy with the idea of Rome as its proper seat – not simply as an idea embodied in the pope himself, but as something that left its imprint on the fabric of the city. Nicholas went further than his immediate predecessors in treating the city of Rome as a kind of project, but he did so in the mould of their intentions, which set about to reconcile the city with the office – Romans with the Curia – and to position Rome as both a spiritual capital and the governing seat of a temporal power, the Papal States. He consequently initiated a series of public works explicitly designed to improve Rome's stature as a city: its inner workings and its standing as a seat of art and learning.

The many thousands of tourists who crowd the piazza facing the recently restored Trevi Fountain (or Fontana di Trevi, 20) each day owe something to the decision taken by Nicholas to repair the Aqua Virgo (Acqua Vergine). This water-supply had been built by Agrippa in the first century BC and was disrupted by the Gothic Wars, when it was used by soldiers to infiltrate the city. When water again started to flow through the aqueduct for the first time in nine centuries, the *mostra* (or fountain) was a rather more modest affair than the eighteenth-century grandiosity we can visit today. Three centuries before Salvi went to work on the monument as it now stands, Leon Battista Alberti conceived of a simple yet elegant basin, with its water source eventually feeding some of Rome's most impressive fountains: those of the Piazza Navona, Piazza Venezia and Piazza di Spagna, (5 the *barca* by Bernini); as well as those of the Piazza del Popolo.

To the reconstruction of the Acqua Vergine we can add numerous cultural accomplishments of the papacy of Nicholas, including the foundation of the great library that would survive as the Vatican Apostolic Library. (By way of balance, he did also lend support to the European slave trade; and witnessed the end of the Eastern Roman Empire with the Ottoman capture of modern-day Istanbul.) His pontificate offered a model of sorts for those who followed. He understood the close relationship that could be fostered between papal power and a well-functioning city: a conflation of temporal and spiritual authority that could extend well beyond the city across the Lands of St Peter as a modern absolutist state.

Of no little import to Nicholas's ambitions was the subtle but effective subjugation of the Capitoline to the Vatican: of the city government to the Curia. In part this was enacted by the Curia's assumption of the responsibility for public buildings, sanitation and water, which had already been difficult to maintain for a small population, but which were straining under the pressure posed by the return of thousands of Church functionaries. As Manfredo Tafuri has argued, this move was already in play during the pontificate of Martin V, but under Nicholas it transmuted into the assumption of direct authority over those magistrates (now paid by the papal treasury) responsible for the various domains of urban management, all the while paying lip service to the city authorities.[1] This was transparent enough that many saw through this shift in the balance of power towards the Curia, but welcome enough, in a way, that it was more tolerated than not. An uprising against papal rule in January 1453 resulted in the would-be Tribune Stefano Porcari swinging by his neck in the Castel Sant'Angelo. His posthumous characterization as Stefano the Proud speaks to Roman ambivalence towards what many would justifiably have regarded as a mode of civic leadership less functional than that offered by the Curia, even if rule by the Church eroded Rome's agency to self-govern. In the words of Alberti (a veritable polymath) in *De Pocari coniuratione* of 1453, the flipside of Nicholan beneficence was that it was no longer legitimate to be Roman above all: 'to be citizens is not permitted'.[2] Romans were now subjects of the Papal States and Rome was their capital. Nicholas saw to it that the Curia absorbed more and more responsibility and, with it, authority over Rome, even connecting for the first time the office of the city's governor to that of the papal Vice Chamberlain (*Vice-Camerlengo*), who was responsible for the possessions of the Holy See. As such, Rome was explicitly and securely recast as a possession of the Church.

The proliferation of the now-ubiquitous pontifical symbol – the crossed keys of St Peter – begins with Nicholas, who introduced it in concord with a programme of urban renewal. This left a visible trace throughout the city on churches both new and renovated, public institutions and infrastructure (such as fountains). It reminded Romans and visitors alike of the good works of the Curia and recalled for the Romans its oversight of Rome as a – *the* – city of the Church.[3]

In restoring Rome to make the city a worthy extension of his office, Nicholas set the tone for the relationship between that office and the city for centuries. At times, as we will shortly see, it was deemed over-extended; at others, it was reluctantly upheld. In *The Art of Religion*, Maarten Delbeke recalls a series of instances in the sixteenth and seventeenth centuries in which the Roman Senate gifted a pope a statue in gratitude for all that he had done for the city, only for it to become a focus of violence and public resistance to the office and figure of the pope as Rome's king-priest upon his death.[4] (By the seventeenth century, Alexander VII knew the pattern well and so delicately declined the offer when his turn came around.) In many important respects, we can lay some blame at the feet of Martin and Nicholas for the absolute identification of the city with the functions and offices headquartered therein and for the challenges this would introduce for Rome at the outset of the modern era.

Nicholas did not breathe new life into the city, then, so much as he manned the bellows on a fire built much earlier, by which means secular institutions fuelled the radiance of the Church and resuscitated the image of Rome as the centre of the world. This was a fragile image, though, and its fragility would permeate the next decades.

## *A Papal City*

Nicholas V set the scene for the surer touch and more expansive imaginations of the sixteenth- and seventeenth-century popes who would follow. He may have been successor to St Peter, but he had the instincts of Rome's secular rulers, rendering the city a papal

territory in terrestrial and administrative as well as
spiritual and symbolic terms, and inviting those who
would assert their temporal power in the Christian
world to recognize the higher authority of the Bishop
of Rome. While Nicholas subjected the city to a *renovatio*, his immediate successors Callixtus III (Borgia) and
Pius II (Piccolomini) were preoccupied with maintain-
ing Rome's authority over a Europe seemingly threat-
ened by the spread of the Ottoman Empire and the
loss of Constantinople to Turkish expansion. For them,
the European extent of Christendom was at stake. But
Sixtus IV (della Rovere) had his attentions on Rome,
renovating the Cappella Magna of the Apostolic Palace
– the aforementioned chapel now named for him and
famed for the frescos painted by Michelangelo under
the patronage of his nephew, Julius II – and advancing
the reorganization of the Borgo initiated by Nicholas V,
with warrens traded for streets allowing for the effi-
cient movement of goods (real power) and processions (symbolic power) between the Vatican hill and
Rome. Alexander VI, who was elevated to the throne
in 1492, restored the Castel Sant'Angelo, constructed
substantial buildings around St Peter's, initiated building works for the University of Rome on the site best
known for its later, seventeenth-century, chapel by
Francesco Borromini (Sant'Ivo alla Sapienza) and subjected the area known as Ortaccio (around the Porta
Ripetta) to urban renewal – even if it soon enough
returned to the more lascivious purposes for which it
had been infamous.

These popes, too, closely identified the city of Rome with a papal principality. Its restoration to a state of glory closely bound up in the image of God-given power and security was a project played out as vigorously on the diplomatic stage (or the battle-field) as on Rome's own fabric. The new dome of St Peter's Basilica serves better than any other instance in the city to concentrate this authority into a single moment. When we pair it, though, with the interventions made by successive popes-as-patrons directly on the ground, in the city's historical centre, we can appreciate the new buildings, public squares, fountains and streets as a programme to reorganize Rome for the needs, above all, of the Curia.

## Two Projects

The project to rebuild St Peter's was already mooted in the time of Nicholas V and addressed the pragmatic issue of an important site of pilgrimage falling into a state of dramatic disrepair. Sustained neglect, long periods of absence and the preference (when in Rome) of the fourteenth- and early fifteenth-century popes for Santa Maria in Trastevere, Santa Maria Maggiore and Santi Apostoli meant that the Basilica of St Peter would likely collapse if left to its own devices. The final paragraphs of Alberti's architectural treatise *De re aed-ificatoria*, dating to the early 1450s, even advance his own technical approach to its patently unstable structure: with a tilting colonnade 'threatening to bring the roof down' and forcing other walls to lean at an angle.[5] Half a century later it was still an issue, and Alexander VI instructed Michelangelo to prepare plans for the restoration of the basilica. Michelangelo would return to this request in time, but it was only with the pope who would effectively serve as Alexander's successor, Julius II, that the project moved forward in earnest, and to the bold designs of the architect Donato Bramante.

Bramante's hand also hovers over via Giulia (27), a major new street realized in concert with his work on St Peter's – and in many ways with the same degree of audacity. St Peter's is a matter of projection, determined by the sheer scale of the dome on the Vatican hill; via Giulia is a less pronounced expression of the papal ego until you realize the force of will required to subjugate an entire neighbourhood of homes, institutions and businesses both by redrawing the map of the city and by recalibrating its focus according to papal dictates. Few of Rome's streets document as clearly as via Giulia does the relationship between the city's fabric and the ambitions of its early modern rulers. It cuts a tangent through that fabric alongside the eastern banks of the Tiber, imposing a new order and efficiency on the working of the zone between the present-day Ponte Sisto (and the Ospedale di Santo Spirito on the opposite bank 8) and, to the north, the Borgo and the seat of papal power. At the crux of this relationship now sits the Florentine church of St John (San Giovanni dei Fiorentini), on which works began during the pontificate of Julius' successor, the Medici pope Leo X, only to be finished two hundred years later. The church is less a cause for the concentration of institutions we now find there so much as it is an index of the local power of the Florentine mercantile community in the neighbourhood of Ponte through which via Giulia cuts. It is no coincidence that here we find the city's major financial institutions, including the Chancellery (Palazzo della Cancelleria, 31) and the Papal Mint (Zecca, 11).

Via Giulia was regularized into Rome's monumental landscape over the centuries, with various institutions (including the Palazzo dei Tribunali, 10, a courthouse, also designed by Bramante) and significant houses built close to it over time – such as, importantly, the Palazzo Farnese (30), which backs on to the street and crosses it by means of a delicate bridge by Michelangelo intended to reach across the Tiber to the Villa Farnesina (28). In 1508, however, when Julius II initiated the project, it offered a base corollary, centred on finance and temporal power, to the processional route taken by Julius Caesar – the Via Triumphalis – and its modern-day equivalent in the Via Papalis (denoting a ceremonial path as well as a functioning street). Papal processions did not take place every day, but when they occurred they reaffirmed a series of relationships in Rome and between the historical city and its youngest, fourteenth *rione* of Borgo, recognizing that papal power had long been traditionally centred on the Lateran Palace rather than on the Vatican. It was, in this sense, a gesture underscored by the specific needs of the early modern papacy.

A series of privileged routes allowed the pope to travel through the city for specific purposes, thereby exercising his authority over Rome – and even today various occasions recall the claim of the pontiff on the city by following historical pathways through its fabric. Crossing the river at the Castel Sant'Angelo, the Holy Father could move along via Recta (or via dei Coronari, 15, running in a straight line towards what would in the 1540s be the Palazzo Chigi, 17), via del Pellegrino (29, leading from the Palazzo dei Tribunali to the Campo dei Fiori (32), where the statue of Giordano Bruno invokes the significance of that path), or via Sistina (13, connecting the Aelian Bridge to via Ripetta) – all to various ends.

The route of the via Papalis (commencing with what is now via dei Banchi Nuovi, 12, and via del Governo Vecchio, 14) connected the Borgo to the Capitoline hill and the seat of urban governance, then on to St John Lateran. Not in any sense a thoroughfare, the via Papalis had been the principal street of late medieval Rome, rather like via Sacra in the age of the Republic or via del Corso today. The houses of the most powerful families lined this street, and it was therefore a centre of trade and politics. It was there that Church and city regularly clashed, sometimes violently, in what Valeria Cafà has called 'a theatre for the conflict of two distinct communities'.[6] There is no coincidence in this route passing by the Piazza di Pasquino (16), on which the dismembered and disfigured third-century BC sculpture for which the square is named became in the sixteenth century a beacon for criticism of the pope, the Curia and the Senate (and, embracing the errors of the government of the day, maintains this role).

Streets were, then, meaningful, and via Giulia was certainly intended to be no less meaningful than via Papalis. It was, and still is, dramatic, the view down its length unimpeded for a full kilometre. Goods could be transported quickly and with minimal risk of loss to thieves, but, more importantly, through its identification with (foreign, non-Roman) banking and the judiciary it symbolically connected the Curia unambiguously to the commercial and political life of Rome. Via Giulia would cut such ancient Roman families as the Orsini and the Colonna out of the picture, undermining their financial authority within the city and recasting Rome's key civic institutions in a papal hue. (In the beautiful book he wrote with Luigi Salerno and Luigi Spezzaferro on the history of this street, Tafuri even commented on the appropriateness of Conrad Hilton building his Cavalieri hotel on the Monte Mario, on an axis with Julius II's unambiguous impression upon the city's historical fabric.)[7] It was a power grab played out with the city as an instrumental material – neither the first, nor the last instance of the same.

Returning now to St Peter's Basilica. As a pair – patron and architect – it is said that the megalomania of Julius and Bramante could not have been better matched. The dome one sees is the work of Michelangelo – or rather Michelangelo and a cast of assistants and successors – but it sits upon a mammoth base that in these same years dramatically amplified the basilica, obliging architects after Bramante to work with the scale he had set in response to the instructions of Julius, which in turn factored in the enormous tomb the della Rovere pontiff had envisioned for himself. (It was eventually installed at San Pietro in Vincoli, 37, in Monti.)

The extent of the amplification to which the Basilica of St Peter was subject in Bramante's hands is easily seen by touring the lower level, in which you can (as noted above) reach out and touch the bases of some of the original columns of the fourth-century structure (still *in situ*) built around the tomb of St Peter. Others have been relocated into the new basilica, as in the *africano* columns that flank the main entrance to the basilica – representing (as Lex Bosman has written) the 'substance of the architecture of the early Christian basilica'.[8] It is a reputational risk to say so, but you can do much worse than to watch Neil Jordan's *The Borgias* (2011–13) to get a sense of the scale and character of the basilica as the fifteenth century ended. The next ten decades' worth of works on this site would result in a structure of properly monumental proportions – a gigantically scaled interior and a dome larger than anything anywhere else in the world. Bramante died in 1514, surviving his patron by a little more than a year, and the building was not realized completely to his centralized, square plan. Instead it sustained elements of designs by Raphael, Giuliano da Sangallo and Baldassare Peruzzi as the years passed. The site remained a live construction zone for a century, but Michelangelo, who reconceptualized Bramante's intentions for the interior by recasting it as a single, coherent volume, thoroughly exceeded them with the scale of his dome.

While we might want to find in this design the stroke of Michelangelo's genius, it is as much a work of many hands as via Giulia turned out to be. It is as complex a work site as any on which you could write. The nave down which you travel to stand underneath the dome is an intervention by Carlo Maderno; and the dome itself was completed not by Michelangelo (who died in 1564, aged 88) but by Domenico Fontana (who oversaw the relocation of the obelisk in its piazza) and Giacomo della Porta, whose most famous building, beyond St Peter's, is Il Gesù – the principal church of the Jesuit movement. Ultimately, the building before which one can stand today, from the perspective of Bernini's piazza, is a façade combining the efforts of Carlo Maderno and Bernini himself, topped by a dome conceived by Michelangelo – determined by a scale devised by Bramante in concert with his pontiff. The last vestiges of the original building survived as late as 1615, when the wall separating the old basilica from the new was finally brought down – more than a century and a half after Alberti had offered his tentative solution to the problem of what is now called Old St Peter's.[9]

## The Sack of 1527

Despite Rome's long history of sustaining or repelling the invasions of numerous enemies, the city had, by the sixteenth century, allowed itself to find comfort in an image of inviolability. The forces of the Holy Roman Emperor Charles V would set the record straight in 1527. Art historian André Chastel sets the renowned cultural and artistic background of the Sack of 1527 as one that 'owed its excitement to an extraordinary convergence of talent, … a frenzy that was intensified by the meeting of individuals and ambitions, to the fervor of a culture that had become self-assured, and to an unusual freedom of speech and behavior'. He speaks of the Clementine style – named for Clement VII, the nephew of the Florentine Lorenzo the Magnificent and first cousin to Leo X – to describe the extraordinary achievements of the decades spanning the turn of the sixteenth century, evidenced in the painting, sculpture and architecture of Raphael, Michelangelo and their contemporaries. But the culture that gave licence in the arts gave licence, too, to a level of corruption and extravagance against which 'criticism … [had] reached a point of no return'.[10]

The sights of Rome's ideologues were set high. Whereas a century earlier, Rome's position as the chief city of the Church – and through it, and still, capital of the world – had been called clearly into doubt, the actions sponsored by the fifteenth-century popes had sought to re-establish Rome as Europe's unassailable spiritual and moral centre. The restitution and realignment of the city's infrastructure was one means towards this end: fountains of potable water, streets, a new port and reinvigorated institutions. Conspicuous support of the arts was another. It is no exaggeration to say that for three and a half centuries Rome lured the most famed artists of the day to study its monuments and ruins, extending its traditions to direct the course of European painting, sculpture and architecture across the early modern age. However, ambition and licence invite irritation and scandal – and this was no more true than in the accusations levelled at the vast centralized administration of the Curia. As Rome's monumental centrepiece, the new fabric of St Peter's was being realized slowly and at an incredible expense. To cover its costs, the Church made a healthy trade in its commodity of choice: indulgences.

An atmosphere of critique had grown around the idea of Rome by the end of the fifteenth century, prompting the Borgia pope Alexander VI to silence the protestations of the Dominican friar Girolamo Savonarola, who had temporarily stripped the Medici of their hold over Florence and called the moral authority of the papacy into question, and also, in 1517, two decades later, prompting Luther to affix (literally or metaphorically) his ninety-five theses to the door of the Wittenburg castle church. This gave rise to a decade of ideological and theological resistance – especially north of the Alps – to the figure of the pontiff and of Rome as the setting of his authority.

The Protestant association of Rome with Babylon dates to this time, and corresponds to a structured resistance to papal power on the part of both the French crown and the Holy Roman Emperor, by whom the pope's own declarations of indefeasibility (1526) had been received poorly. It led to military aggression by papal forces and resistance by Charles V, whose barely controllable army on the Italian peninsula was commanded by Charles III, Duke of Bourbon – a reprise of the French descent towards Naples in 1494, which had left Rome unscathed, but which in 1527 had an altogether different outcome. Politics and diplomacy were overtaken by baser instincts on the path south through Italy, and the lure of Roman riches kept the Caroline army moving. The promise of indemnity was not tempting enough to prevent an attack, and one after the other the Leonine Wall was breached around the Borgo and Vatican (6 May 1527), then the Aurelian Wall around Trastevere and, finally, the Ponte Sisto was crossed into Campo Marzio and Rome was thoroughly plundered. Clement fled, disguised as a bishop, and with three thousand people took refuge in the Castel Sant'Angelo. (As a matter of scale, the 1526 census had Rome's population at only 53,000.)

The assault on the teachings and practices of the Church and the authority of the Bishop of Rome flanked a disastrous decade for the office of the papacy and, now, for the city as its conscious embodiment. By 1527, the Protestant Reformation had crystallized across the north of Europe. The breach by Charles de Bourbon was, for many, little more than a welcome confirmation of the end of Roman universalism.

The Sack was not merely a posture: it did real damage, and for a long time. A memoir recorded by one of Charles's commanders starts to invoke the damage: six thousand men killed, houses plundered and 'a good portion of the town' put to the flame; the city infested with plague from all the unburied bodies, from both sides; a pope forced to surrender his stronghold; artworks defaced; and after the aggressors returned from their escape from the hot Roman summer, a six-month period of systematic pillaging across the winter of 1527–8, during which Pope Clement licked his wounds in Orvieto.[11] One correspondent was moved to write: 'It is no longer Rome but Rome's grave.'[12] Relics were disfigured and the most holy sites of the city were subject to profanity. It would take the election of the Farnese pope Paul III in 1534, a triumphal procession by a victorious yet supplicant Charles V himself through Rome (April 1536) and the better part of a century to reinstate Rome's art, treasures and stature to their proper place. 'The Church reaffirmed her authority,' Chastel concludes. 'Rome regained the prestige that was at the same time ancient and Christian, cultural and religious.' Meanwhile, Charles, 'celebrating his victory over infidels and heretics', was 'conclusively exonerated ... of responsibility for the sack, and placed ... in the ranks of the great emperors'.[13] Rome was bruised, but lived to fight another day.

## A Slow Transition

The undisputed dominion of the new Basilica of St Peter over the city happened neither quickly nor smoothly. The architect of its fabric and nature of his intentions changed frequently, and some centuries passed from the time when some form of intervention in this sacred but dilapidated structure seemed inevitable to the moment when the grand piazza of the new basilica could command a monumental vista reaching as far as the Castel Sant'Angelo. An engraving by Giovanni Battista de' Cavalieri helpfully disrupts the notion that the symbolic claim made over Rome by the dome of St Peter's offered any kind of scenography to the slow transition from a Rome as the city of an absent pontiff to a properly papal Rome in which all things became, one way or another, subject to the Holy See. Cavalieri depicts the state of the Basilica of St Peter during celebrations of the Holy Year of

1575, more than a decade after Michelangelo's death, in which 300,000 people came to Rome (figure 4.2). Only with the supernatural clarity of foresight could one have imagined the events presaging the Council of Trent (1545–63) at the time St Peter's Basilica drew the attentions of Julius II. By 1575, though, the Council had been concluded for over a decade and the implementation of curial policies to combat the effects of the Protestant Reformation was being felt across the city under the efforts of Pope Gregory XIII. The Holy Year was one such event.

The more permanent wave of baroque churches and piazzas would follow in the decades to come, recasting Rome so definitively that it is possible to forget that the ideas, institutions and interventions of the fifteenth and sixteenth centuries did not result in an immediate change from one state in the history of the city to another.

Remarkably, Cavalieri depicts the state of the reconstruction of St Peter's as an amalgam of two distinct buildings – invoking two equally distinct epochs. The fourth-century basilica still rests on the foundations laid in the rule of Constantine (denoted in his drawing with the words Porticus Constantiniana), flanked on one side by the Apostolic Palace and on the other by the Domus Archipresbyteri Basilicae (home of the cardinate 'arciprete' of St Peter's), with two levels of medieval construction extending up the original, if not insubstantial, basilica. But it is the drum of the *Fabrica S Petri Basilicæ Nova* rising up from its rear

**Figure 4.2:** Giovanni Battista de' Cavalieri, *The Ceremony of the Opening of the Porta Santa for the Jubilee of 1575, with Crowds of Pilgrims Standing in the Piazza San Pietro with the New Cathedral Rising behind the Old One*, engraving, 1575.

that invokes the image of St Peter's we might well imagine to have tracked Rome's rebirth in these centuries. Most significantly, the dome is still missing, and would still be so in depictions of the coronation of Sixtus V a decade after the Holy Year – a reminder that despite Michelangelo's singular role in conceiving of this most iconic Catholic structure (it no longer seems proper to call it Roman), it was a work of several generations and many hands. From the reign of Sixtus, it would take another four popes to get the dome up and its crucifix mounted – in reality fifteen years or so, traversing some very brief pontificates – and another two pontiffs to see the fabric of the old church dismantled and the new building more or less completed (under Paul V), even if it would for another two centuries be the subject of endless proposals for further modification.

The road, then, from the first tentative reclamations of Eugene IV and Martin V to the completion of the grand piazza of Bernini with which this chapter began is not one of natural rebirth or of the welcome flourishing of the offices of the Church on Roman soil. It is, instead, a steady and far from certain negotiation between the Curia and the Capitoline, the largely foreign administrative population of the Holy See (who thought themselves the natural citizens of a higher-order Rome) and the people of Rome – those who were not Florentines or Venetians or Genovese residents of the Holy City, but citizens with a deep historical claim on the city as their own.

## A Rhetorical Renewal

On his deathbed, Nicholas V had summed up the role that could be taken by an ecclesiastical building programme. While the masses, he argued, meaning the Romans, were largely ignorant of the reasoning that placed absolute authority on the shoulders of the Church, on occasion they could hear its well-read officers explain why this was so. 'Yet they need to be impressed by grand spectacles: without these their piety – which rests on unstable, even fragile foundations – will disappear as time passes.' The buildings of the Church, he asserted, can 'reinforce a popular faith based on learned assumptions' – and is the 'only way to maintain and foster piety and perpetuate it with laudable devotion'.[14] The Council of Trent prompted a vast programme of artistic production intended to complement renewed efforts to make fresh converts in every corner of the world, drawing lost souls back to Rome and confirming for those who remained faithful the universality of their Church. It placed display and the art of rhetoric firmly at the centre of Catholic culture, encouraging believers to stay put and those without Christianity to draw closer to its brightest beacon. Alexander VI had divided vast territories between Spanish and Portuguese crowns, and together with lands across Asia (both acquired and desired) the newly formed Society of Jesus followed the colonial path to bring the new message of the Church to the farthest reaches of the earth – with seventeenth- and eighteenth-century missions extending to eastern Asia, Africa, Oceania and the Americas.

Its missions placed Rome at the centre of a new global geography. Of the city's two principal Jesuit churches, Il Gesù (34), at the eastern end of the Corso Vittorio Emanuele II (and on the path once followed by via Papalis), takes precedence as the Society's mother church. But its sibling, named for St Ignatius Loyola (Sant'Ignazio, 18), offers the more unrestrained display of rhetoricality as it connects the Catholic world to the heavens and reasserts Rome's centrality as its earthly locus. The church building, designed by a largely forgotten figure named Giovanni Tristano, is located near the Pantheon and originally served as the chapel of the Collegio Romano (19), established through a sixteenth-century gift to the Loyolite Order by the Marchesa Vittoria della Tolfa (of the Orsini family) to enable the Society to better pursue its mission. Working to a modest budget, members of the Order constructed the edifice themselves; a model of the original design is even now on display in the church foyer. It was not built to plan, however, and the generous dome intended for the crossing of the nave and transept was never constructed. A lack of monies instead prompted a now famous trick of the eye by the Trentine painter, architect and Jesuit priest Andrea Pozzo, who installed a *quadrattura* fresco to extend the interior of the church into a false dome. He likewise executed the large ceiling mural shown here (figure 4.3), depicting the apotheosis of Sant'Ignazio surrounded by allegories of Europe, Asia, Africa and America, the ceiling extending up into the heavens, into which the saint is borne by a host of angelic creatures. It is not subtle; nor is it intended to be.

## Barberini and Beyond

To this famous ceiling we can pair another painted in these same years, balancing out the missionary zeal of Sant'Ignazio with a reassuring reminder of the determination of the ecclesiastical dynasty. On the northern slope of the Quirinal hill sits the Palazzo Barberini, built for Maffeo Barberini to the design of Carlo Maderno – whose importance to the histories of art and architecture is often overshadowed by his assistants, Gianlorenzo Bernini and Francesco Borromini, and the story of their decades-long baroque rivalry. On Maderno's death in 1629, the commission to design Palazzo Barberini (7) was given to Bernini to complete, and it will have to suffice, here, to direct attention to a pair of staircases at either end of the building's ceremonial façade, by Bernini and Borromini, respectively, as a nod to their fascinating story. It is tracked, too (since we are in the neighbourhood), in the pair of churches we noted at the very outset of this book, Bernini's Sant'Andrea al Quirinale and Borromini's San Carlo alle Quattro Fontane (22, 23) – two churches that, though modest in scale, are of great artistic

**Figure 4.3:** Andrea Pozzo, *The Apotheosis of St Ignatius*, ceiling fresco, 1691–4. Church of Sant'Ignazio di Loyola.

significance. In 1623, Barberini acquired the right to reside in the Quirinal Palace (21) with his ascension to the *Cathedra Petri* as Urban VIII, in doing so taking the summer palace initiated by Gregory XII in 1583 and turning it into the seat of the pope's power as monarch of the Papal States – a temporal complement to the Apostolic Palace. Urban's pontificate lasted for more than two decades at a crucial moment in which the Church built prolifically: extending the suite of colleges and congregations through which it pursued its mission; and constructing grand spectacles worthy of the effort expended by those who made the pilgrimage to Rome in these years.

The proliferation throughout Rome of his family emblem, the three bees of the Barberini, combined with the crossed keys of St Peter, is a potent reminder of the import of this family for Rome in the second quarter of the seventeenth century. The ceiling fresco of the great hall of the Palazzo Barberini (figure 4.4) was painted by the 'prince' (*Principe*) of the Accademia di San Luca, Rome's academy of the arts: Pietro da Cortona, whose Church of Santi Luca e Martini, on the Forum, we have likewise met earlier in these pages, and who, together with Bernini and Borromini, is regularly named as one of the masters of the Roman baroque. Like the ceiling at Sant'Ignazio, the *Allegory of Divine Providence* is an allegory of the power of the Barberini: a composition of angelic figures and emblematic bees suspended in a space reaching up towards the heavens; the crown remarking upon the

**Figure 4.4:** Pietro da Cortona, *Allegory of Divine Providence and Barberini Power*, ceiling fresco, 1633–9. Palazzo Barberini.

achievement of Urban VIII, while the shaky foundations of Divine Providence and the rapacious appetite
of Time put good circumstance into perspective.

Rome has always been a city of great families,
and the sheer volume of new buildings, fountains
and institutions, elaborate restorations, recalibrated
public square and rejuvenated streets across the seventeenth century saw their mark left clearly on its
monuments: the Nicholan device of the papal keys,
with their claim of the dominion of St Peter's successor over Rome, extended to the rule of specific families, historically Roman and otherwise. The families
of Chigi, Barberini, Borghese, Pamphili and Farnese
took Rome's reigns, one after the other, and built,
and built. The Chigi gave the Church Alexander VII
(with his crest of the six mountains and a star); the
Barberini (and their bees) Urban VIII; the Borghese
Paul V (whose emblem was the dragon); the Pamphili
Innocent X (the dove and olive twig); and the Farnese
Paul III (the *fleurs de lys*). Their estates gave form
to the unbuilt edges of the city. Properties like the
Villa Borghese and Villa Doria-Pamphili came to be
acquired by the city as modern public parks. (Urban
VIII exemplifies the ambivalence of these figures
towards what we might now regard as the inevitable
embrace of modern reason by this office: his fame as
a city-maker will forever be overshadowed by his trial
of Galileo Galilei in 1633 – whose positions he well
understood, but whose faith in science he ultimately
could not countenance.)

Another setting for the theatre of the Barberini dynasty offers a counterpoint to its grandeur and its implied permanence while confirming the frailty of ambition. The crypt of Santa Maria della Concezione (6), the church of the Capuchin order, is among the more challenging sites you can encounter in even a short visit to Rome. The church was built between 1626 and 1631 on Ludovisi land under Urban's authority and to the design of Antonio Felice Casoni on what is today via Vittorio Veneto. It contains paintings by Guido Reni, Lanfranco and Pietro da Cortona, but its unique place in the Roman churchscape is owed to the crypt.

As befits such a powerful and hugely nepotistic family, Pope Urban's younger brother, Antonio (the Elder) Barberini, was head of the Capuchin order and one of four Barberini raised to the cardinalate on his election. The relatively unassuming Capuchin church, then, is one of a series of monuments to this family's achievements in very close proximity to one another. The Quirinale and the Palazzo Barberini may be a testament to power, but the crypt of Santa Maria della Concezione recalls its fragility. Admittedly, there is nothing modest about the efforts made to establish the ossuary you encounter in the Capuchin crypt. Its eighteenth-century compositions make use of the remains of more than three thousand members of the order (exhumed and carted around the Quirinal hill from a friary on via dei Lucchesi). They include vertebral chandeliers and skeletal members of the brotherhood either in meditative repose or on silent watch, all framed by a rococo sensitivity towards the ornamental possibilities of the human frame. Its five bays are lined with soil imported from Jerusalem. In the first of these a *memento mori* recalls the ubiquity and inevitability of the great equalizer. An intact skeleton is suspended from the ceiling in the manner of death, scales and scythe to the ready – a Barberini, as it happens, in the person of a young eighteenth-century princess of the family. It is, in one sense, a monument to a dynasty at the height of its powers, but pays tribute, more importantly, to the imperatives to be devout.

## A Monument in the Making

By the eighteenth century and the era of the Grand Tour, Rome had transformed from one kind of spectacle to another, from the setting for a live enactment of the glories of the Church – the ground zero of Counter-Reformation – to a city become ruin. This was the Romantic Rome to which poets, painters and the moneyed were drawn. The most widely collected views of Rome were, without doubt, drawn by the hand of Giovanni Battista Piranesi, an architect of Venetian origin whose critical fortunes have been shaped by his gifts as a *vedutista* (views artist). Few libraries of substance are without a number of Piranesi's etchings or drawings – their diffusion is startlingly universal, to the point that his views of monuments contemporary with his own world are instantly recognizable. The tradition of making etched views for print is not at all new, but the scale and message of the perspective views produced by Piranesi are without competitor. His most famous predecessor was Giuseppe Vasi, whose prolific production is often, but unfairly, overlooked. But whereas Vasi drew what he saw, Piranesi's vistas of Rome (and studies, often highly technical, of its ruins) eerily combine an archaeologist's penchant for precision with the artist's imagination. With his stylus he immortalized such monuments as the Pantheon (as we saw in the Introduction, figure 0.3), the Colosseum and the Forum Romanum as ruins in the making. To modern eyes this might seem overly imaginative – Thomas De Quincey even accused him, in 1821, of opium abuse[15] – but in the eight-eenth-century city, visited by scores of young men of means within the itinerary of their classical educa-tion *in situ*, Rome had indeed witnessed its ancient monuments falling into a state of ruination. This was a consequence not understood as such over the centuries: disused buildings were raided for their materials, and a temple in the *disabitato* would not be maintained for the sake of preservation alone. In Piranesi's shadows we see an appeal to Rome's eternal glory that recognizes its loose hold on the present. And in the rising chaos at the forefront of each image, one senses the irreversible nature of time's passage.

Piranesi's production was large. It had to be, because

not only was he an avid documentarian of his adopted city – scrabbling around digs with archaeologists of the French Academy – but he used his stylus to fight for that same city and its illustrious past – which was, for him, palpable in its present. In his early Roman years, in the mid-1740s, Piranesi had contributed to the vast project to draw a grand plan of Rome, led by Giambattista Nolli – the *Piànta Grande di Roma*. This drawing offers a snapshot of the extent of the city's streets and buildings without regard to their relative age or style; and it offers an account of those buildings whose interiors functioned in the realm of the urban. It is a document of Rome, public and private. More than this, though, it offers a sense of Rome's density as a city, and of Rome as a modern city. (It is not coincidental that maps of historical or medieval Rome tend to overlay these somewhat foreign pasts over Nolli's documentation.) This map, importantly, is not a stage on which artefacts parade. They are instead entrenched in the mesh of a city replete with incongruities: medieval and modern, ancient and medieval.

It follows, then, that in his own graphic production Piranesi offered up image after image of the city as it stood, immersed in its own history. He draws the Pantheon, or the Baths of Diocletian, or the Golden House of Nero (the Domus Aurea, figure 4.5), *as he sees them*, which is to say not exactly as another might see them. These are no objective documents. They draw you into the idea of Rome as a mighty and eternal force handed down from a glorious antiquity

**Figure 4.5:** Giovanni Battista Piranesi, View of the Remains of the Dining Room of the Golden House of Nero, *Vedute di Roma* (1778).

and which lent credence and gave momentum to the authority found by the Church (and an emerging idea of western civilization) in the city's ancient past.

Drawing was, for Piranesi, not the end game – he was, after all, an architect, and he sought many opportunities to build. He missed on numerous occasions the role of Architect to the Fabric of St Peter's, which would have endorsed him as a figure for the canon. His main legacy in stone, however, is the substantial enlargement of a tenth-century Benedictine monastery into a small priory church realized under the papacy of a fellow Venetian, the Rezzonico pope Clement XIII, whose nephew, Cardinal Giambattista

Rezzonico, headed the Order of Malta. Located at the top of the Aventine hill, close to Santa Sabina, Piranesi's Santa Maria del Priorato (39) is a curious study in the stripped-back language of academic classicism and the rich world of emblems, invoking an unmediated antiquity as it celebrates the fashions of his present. The gardens of the adjacent villa figure all too briefly in *La grande bellezza*, the dome of St Peter's flashing into view before Gambardella puts their famous keyhole to use at the start of a night of privileged access to the treasures of contemporary Rome. That these treasures are the legacy, too, of these centuries of rebuilding Rome as the centre of an empire should not, by now, surprise us. St Peter's is a monument in the making, framed by Piranesi as much as by the ambitions of its patron. And as it goes for St Peter's over the course of these centuries, so it goes for Rome entire.

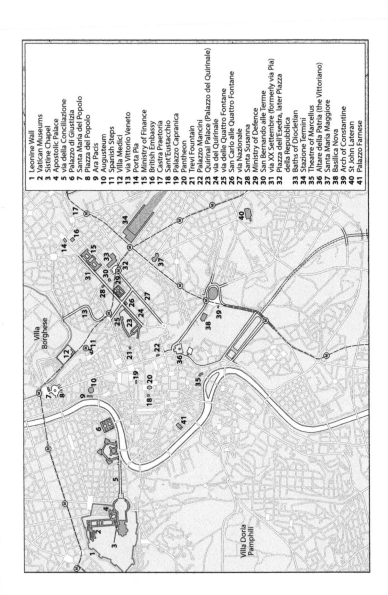

1 Leonine Wall
2 Vatican Museums
3 Sistine Chapel
4 Apostolic Palace
5 via della Conciliazione
6 Palazzo di Giustizia
7 Santa Maria del Popolo
8 Piazza del Popolo
9 Ara Pacis
10 Augusteum
11 Spanish Steps
12 Villa Medici
13 via Vittorio Veneto
14 Porta Pia
15 Ministry of Finance
16 British Embassy
17 Castra Praetoria
18 Sant'Eustacchio
19 Palazzo Capranica
20 Pantheon
21 Trevi Fountain
22 Palazzo Mancini
23 Quirinal Palace (Palazzo del Quirinale)
24 via del Quirinale
25 via delle Quattro Fontane
26 San Carlo alle Quattro Fontane
27 via Nazionale
28 Santa Susanna
29 Ministry of Defence
30 San Bernardo alle Terme
31 via XX Settembre (formerly via Pia)
32 Piazza dell'Esedra, later Piazza della Repubblica
33 Baths of Diocletian
34 Stazione Termini
35 Theatre of Marcellus
36 Altare della Patria (the Vittoriano)
37 Santa Maria Maggiore
38 Basilica Nova
39 Arch of Constantine
40 St John Lateran
41 Palazzo Farnese

Villa Borghese

Villa Doria Pamphili

# The Capital of Italy

*Behind the Porta Pia – A Symbol of European Power
– Planning for a Modern Republic – Roma Caput
Italia – The Roman Question – Romanità – Open
City – From the Foro Mussolini to the XVII Olympiad
– Housing the Romans – I grandi progetti*

## Behind the Porta Pia

The intersection of via del Quirinale with via delle Quattro Fontane (25) sits at the top of the rise of the Quirinal hill and is, as the street name suggests, marked out by four fountains that date to the sixteenth century. Given the traffic that hurtles through this crossroads, you take your own life in your hands by falling prey to the temptation to snap the sculptures of the rivers Tiber and Aniene (or Teverone) and the goddess Juno, designed by Domenico Fontana, or Pietro da Cortona's Diana. The undulating façade of Francesco Borromini's seventeenth-century Trinitarian church (26) into which 'the Tiber' is embedded – a façade executed by his nephew after his untimely death – is likewise an inviting shot. The postcard images are hard to replicate, though, without the right lenses or access to the buildings that face on to the intersection, and the footpaths hardly deserve the name; thus the intolerance of the passing traffic becomes an apt reminder of the intersection, too, of Rome's monumental life with the regular comings and goings of those who call the city home. Following the street that runs towards the north-east, away from the now presidential Quirinal Palace (Palazzo del Quirinale, 23), you pass the hulking neoclassical masses of the Ministries of Defence, (29) and, a block later, Finance (15), between which sits, on the left, the turn-of-the-seventeenth-century church of Santa Susanna designed by Carlo Maderno (28, where on occasion you can top up on second-hand English books), and on the right the little round church of San Bernardo alle Terme (30, named for the nearby Baths of Diocletian). Further along the street, the city to your back, the post-war British Embassy (designed by Sir Basil Spence, 16) opens out to the right on this walk, which brings you to the Aurelian Wall and the Porta Pia (14) (figure 5.1) – rebuilt by Michelangelo after the Sack of Rome of 1527 and enlarged in a works campaign that concluded in 1869. To arrive at the Porta Pia is to arrive, too, at the site on which Rome, one year later, conceded its fate to the nascent Kingdom of Italy.

Rome entered the modern age as a city at the centre of two worlds: one extending to the farthest reaches of the earth, riding waves of Spanish and Portuguese colonization that secured Catholic Europe's modern

**Figure 5.1:** The Porta Pia after the breach of the Aurelian Wall (damage to the right side of the image), September 1870.

fortunes; the other spreading north and south from Lazio, bordered at the end of the eighteenth century by the Kingdom of Sicily and the Duchy of Modena, the Grand Duchy of Tuscany, French-occupied Lombardy and, in the far north, the Republic of Venice: that is, the Papal States, of which the pope was monarch. It entered the nineteenth century, too, as an embodiment of antiquity and a setting for connecting, through travel and the sojourn, a secular appreciation of both the ancient and early modern worlds. (Many of those who were thus drawn to Rome in the nineteenth and twentieth centuries in search of an encounter with the profound depths of Rome's history found their final resting place in the *cimitero acattolico*, with which we concluded the second chapter.)

The street that ends with Michelangelo's ceremonial gateway was once, obviously enough, called via Pia (31). It is now named for the skirmish on 20 September 1870, in which the papal army half-heartedly confronted that of a unified Italy. With Garibaldi's march north from Sicily in 1860 to meet the Savoyard forces from Piedmont, the Papal States had already, by that time, been thoroughly compromised and the territories ruled by Pius IX much diminished. Rome itself remained intact, but as a geo-political island. Founded in March 1861, the newly constituted parliament of the Kingdom of Italy declared Rome its capital nearly a decade before the fall of the Papal States, more than clearly forecasting its intentions to bring the Holy See and Rome into the Italian fold – and reiterating the city's seemingly inevitable right to rule. The nineteenth-century European power landscape was nothing if not a moving feast, and while France had maintained a state of enmity with the Papal States across the century's first decades, by 1860 Napoleon III had committed troops to protect Rome's independence from a unified Italy. The declaration of war with the Kingdom of Prussia in July 1870 saw those troops redeployed without sufficient diplomatic protections being put in place, and Rome was consequently exposed to the march of history.

The Italian king Vittorio Emanuele (Victor Emanuel) II presented Pius IX with terms that would have made for a peaceful entry of his troops into the city and secured a pact between Italy and the Holy See.

This would have allowed Rome to remain the centre in perpetuity of the Catholic world, recognizing the pope's spiritual authority at the head of the Church, but removing his temporal power as a head of state, rendering him an Italian subject. With these terms refused, Rome was placed under a brief siege that ended with more of a whimper than a bang and the breach of the ancient Aurelian Wall to one side of the Porta Pia. The pope had already withdrawn to the Apostolic Palace (4) at the Vatican, behind the Leonine Wall, and within a couple of weeks, and with the absence of his influence, the Roman citizenry voted to join Italy. This effectively dissolved the Papal States and left the Vatican as an unofficial enclave within the city it once called its own. The papal palace on Quirinal hill became the official residence of the Italian kings and, decades later, the President of the Republic. This relegation of the pontiff to the standing of *Captivus Vaticani* was not part of the battle plan so much as a consequence of Pius refusing to bend his knee. Those who followed him on St Peter's Throne also took this stance, hence the vexed Roman Question: how to accommodate the Holy See as the centre of a global community of Catholics with important alliances throughout Europe, Asia and the Americas, while asserting Italian sovereignty over Rome as the capital of a modern nation? It would take more than half a century to resolve, with the Lateran Treaty in 1929 granting sovereignty to the Vatican City as a state distinct from the Holy See.

## A Symbol of European Power

In the nineteenth-century trade of empires for kingdoms and republics, Rome remained at the centre of
a thorny problem – its territorial sovereignty provi-
sionally guaranteed by alliances forged between the
Papal States and Catholic powers and its spiritual sovereignty projected from the *cathedra* of the Bishop of
Rome.

In Rome's own historical trajectory from republic
to empire and in its seemingly unassailable centrality
to the Catholic world, it offered a lesson for France,
which had emerged as one of the strongest European
powers of the early nineteenth century. Rome was
largely impotent, however, in the face of Napoleonic
ambition and France's conditional enthusiasm for
the Risorgimento (Italy's unification movement). In
his *History of the Decline and Fall of the Roman Empire*
(1776–89), Edward Gibbon suggested that the Roman
Empire unwound in the face of the rise of Christianity
and the increased challenge posed from beyond its
edges. At the start of the modern age, Rome now confronted different kinds of evangelists and barbarians
of another stripe: the proponents of unification, on
the one hand, with their vision of a Rome unfettered
by the Curia; and the armies of the French Republic,
on the other, imagining the authority that would come
from the conquest of this ancient imperial capital. In
both these ambitions, the battle between Rome's fabric
and the idea of Rome remained a live issue.

Napoleon Bonaparte had been born little more than 300 kilometres from Rome in Ajaccio, Corsica, and in the wake of the Revolution that commenced in 1789 he followed a path that placed him at the head of the army that invaded Italy (1796–7) with a view to diminishing the power of Habsburg Austria and the last vestiges of the Holy Roman Empire. This began a decades-long involvement of French forces south of the Alps and placed the various kingdoms, republics and duchies of Italy at the mercy of a territorial contest between the French and Habsburg empires and their various allies. Napoleon invaded the Papal States in 1798, and his Chief of Staff, Louis-Alexandre Berthier, took Rome that year to establish a short-lived Roman Republic that obliged Pius VI into an exile from which he never returned. Following a six-month interregnum (and a conclave held in Venice), Pius VII was appointed his successor, and he restored the Papal States to the Holy See (not coincidentally also travelling to Paris in 1804 for Napoleon's coronation). But over the course of the Napoleonic Wars – however one resolves the fuzziness of their chronology – the Papal States, and Rome at their centre, remained in French sights, and even Pius VII found himself in exile for a six-year spell from 1809 due to the French annexation of his territories.

The Académie de France à Rome is an apt marker of French interests in the ancient city. It was relocated in 1803 to the sixteenth-century Villa Medici (12), on the edge of the now public gardens of the

Villa Borghese, a short distance from the Spanish Steps (11). One of many foreign academies scattered throughout the city, it had originally occupied the fifteenth-century Palazzo Capranica (19), just a short street away from the Pantheon and, since 1737, the Palazzo Mancini on via del Corso (22), which had been repurposed as the French Embassy to the Holy See after the French Revolution. Moving the French Academy to this parkland setting sent a number of clear signals – the Roman headquarters (historically speaking) of the powerful Medici aligned Napoleon with another (Tuscan) family that had entered Rome from outside its establishment and exerted a substantial influence over the city's arts, culture and institutions. (The other significant sixteenth-century palace housing a major French institution in Rome is the Palazzo Farnese (41), with its beautiful Michelangelo-designed cornice, although this dates from a gift made nation to nation in 1936.)

### Planning for a Modern Republic

Alongside the adaptation of a number of Rome's more prominent *palazzi* to new ends across the early and mid-nineteenth century, several public works projects in these same decades gave shape to civic values that derived from French lessons in urban planning. One should not assume from his surname that Giuseppe Valadier was himself French (although his family was of Provençal stock), but he went further than most in giving scale and character to the various stages of Rome's public life. He redesigned the piazza around the Trevi Fountain (21) and oversaw the installation of the parklands running along the Aurelian Wall from the Basilica of St John Lateran (40) to Santa Croce in Gerusalemme. Most prominent of his works, though, is his intervention in the Piazza del Popolo (8).

Valadier enacted a series of changes to the northern entrance to Rome, reflecting the monumental impulse that then accompanied many republican projects and the influence of French urban planning. (Consider the conception by Pierre Charles L'Enfant of Washington's National Mall in the 1790s; or, decades later, Baron Haussmann's role in the reconstruction of Paris under Napoleon III.) The modern reconfiguration of the Piazza del Popolo dates to a 1772 student competition held by the Accademia di San Luca, which amounted to nothing, but sought to solve the problem of an ill-composed public square that had not proven itself to be up to the task of offering a monumental welcome to the city. This is not to suggest an absence of earlier schemes for the piazza. Alexander VII had paid it careful attention as the baroque setting for the church of Santa Maria del Popolo (7), which was deeply connected to his own family. But attitudes towards urban planning change over time, and the baroque stage gave way to the clean sight-lines and regular form of the French fashions of the day.

Valadier seized on the stalled momentum of the earlier competition to make a proposal, in 1794, to place barracks at the city gate. The project spanned the years of French occupation and the exile of Pius VI, and over that time Valadier revised his scheme to reference the shape of the piazza designed by Bernini for St Peter's Basilica while introducing a landscaped promenade up the steep rise of the Pincian hill, immediately to the east. Rather than maintain the church of Santa Maria del Popolo as the symbolic focus of the piazza, Valadier's moves – which included the barracks – gave the streets themselves a monumental character, reinforced by a clearly legible geometry, symmetry and long views into key parts of the Campo Marzio. When Pius VII entered the city to reclaim the *cathedra* abandoned by his predecessor more than a decade and a half earlier in 1814 (the year of Napoleon's abdication), he passed through Valadier's construction site. It remains, even today, a monument to French taste in a Roman setting, and to Rome's accommodation, once more, of foreign interests within the imbrications of its ancient fabric.

## Roma Caput Italia

The relocation of the Italian capital from Florence to Rome in 1870 brought about major changes to the city's makeup and needs. Rome may have contained a million people at its imperial prime (and perhaps half as many again, since estimates vary wildly), but when it was inherited by Nicholas V in the 1440s it was a city of just fifty thousand or so people. Despite Rome's importance over the early modern era, it remained sparsely populated, compared, at least, with its density in the age of empire, even as the unification movement spilled over the Aurelian Wall into the heart of the Papal States. Even then, the pope commanded only around 200,000 subjects, 10 per cent of the population of Paris at that time. In the century following Italian unification, however, Rome grew more than four-fold, in part reflecting the influx of functionaries needed to run the government and civil service of the Kingdom of Italy and in part tracking the increased urbanization of the Italian population as a whole across the twentieth century's first decades – a response to industrialization, economic crises and conflict with a flood of fishermen and farmers entering Rome and Naples and the factory cities of the north. As a result, for the first time in its history, the Aurelian Wall could no longer contain the people of Rome, and the walls of the Italian capital went the way of those of numerous European cities and ceded to suburban expansion. It was a fitting consequence to mark, too, the fundamental change in the city's very nature, now sitting as it was at the centre of a modern nation rather than as the centre of an ecclesiastical kingdom.

This expansion would play out over several decades. With the introduction in 1871 of civic self-government in the setting of national rule, Rome was rhetorically subject to a number of significant changes in its governance and status. But as urban historian Spiro Kostof has observed, these were largely a recasting of well-established hierarchies that meant the 'wresting of Rome from papal rule' was something of 'a sham':

> The national government ensured the continuing existence of a privileged class which lived at the expense of the people. Free enterprise helped to enlarge the scope of this ruling class, but there was no true difference in the social substructure. The Church retained its hold by supplanting feudal territoriality with capitalism. As for the image of resurgent glory, that too was shaped with total indifference to the interests of the common man. Where the profit and convenience of the ruling class made it expedient, the past was summarily sacrificed. Patrician villas vanished under the developer's grid – and with them vanished the people's green. Where the decorum of the ruling class demanded the isolation of ancient relics, or ample avenues cut through the older fabric, it was common people and their unhealthy tenements that were found to be standing in the way.[1]

The notion of a 'Third Rome' emerges from this time: encapsulating a desire for the new Italian state to follow in the footsteps of the emperors and popes, and, as the nineteenth-century republicanist Giuseppe Mazzini put it in 1849, to render Rome a city for the people. Three urban development plans were drafted – in 1873, 1883 and 1909 – that systematically drew the lines of Rome's expansion and zoning to encourage it to behave as a modern city. But as much as they described how Rome might grow within and beyond its traditional boundaries, the burden of countless monuments and sites of historical importance or archaeological significance demanded a continued negotiation between the immediate and future needs of that rapidly evolving modern city and the imperative to preserve the relics of the past on which and around which it was built. The paths of many of Rome's most important streets date to these urban planning efforts, as does the appearance of many of the city's monuments and archaeological sites. The exposure of the Largo Argentina, which we encountered in Chapter 2, pointedly recalls the archaeological levels of the ancient city exposed by the public works of these decades, while the disappearance of vast tracts of worker housing or unremarkable historical fabric is an intentioned absence that barely registers in our present-day experience of the city.

Kostof again perfectly sums up the problem of the view of history that contemporary Rome allows. 'We do not recall enough', he wrote in 1973,

> that what we see and study of the architectural history of Rome has been selected, cleaned up and staged for us by the planners and rulers of the Third Rome. They were the ones who decided which past buildings were worthy of preservation, and which expendable for the sake of Progress; how much of excavated antiquity

would be retained for show, and how much quickly buried again under paving or new construction.[2]

One of the first gestures by Rome's new municipal council was to carve the appropriately named via Nazionale (27) through centuries' worth of buildings and street patterns to connect the Baths of Diocletian – and, before it, the Piazza dell'Esedra, and what would in the 1880s become the Piazza della Repubblica (32) – to the Capitoline hill. It was a gesture akin to that made by Julius II. A modern street for a modern city.

The regulatory plan of 1873 provided for the swathes of residential zones that define the contemporary city in the neighbourhoods north of Castel Sant'Angelo and the Vatican, south of the Aventine hill on the Monte Testaccio, in new blocks around the ancient military camp of the Castra Praetoria (17, the neighbourhood of Castro Pretorio, around the national library) and all around the Stazione Termini (34). The map identified those areas that would require demolition to make way for the major new thoroughfares and traffic routes that did not yet have Roman motorists in mind, but which would form the basis of their experience in the decades to come.

A period of astonishing growth meant that a revised plan was produced a mere decade later, a plan that reinforced these gestures but extended them north of the Piazza del Popolo into the new neighbourhood of Flaminio, leading towards what are now the sites of the 1960 Olympic Village and the National Museum of the 21st-Century Arts, MAXXI. It furthermore rationalized those parts of the city marked out for urban expansion into the comparably more regular grids that give a certain rhythm to the experience of dragging luggage in any direction from Termini. Recalling the rhetorical move made by Julius II in siting his law courts on via Giulia, the plan of 1883 (figure 5.2) set aside land adjacent to the Castel Sant'Angelo for the hulking great Palazzo di Giustizia – the Palace of Justice (6), known also by the derogative name of 'Il palazzaccio' to denote its bulky and brutish appearance.

By 1909, the area around Piazza Mazzini had realized the ambitions of its namesake, with modern city grids and radial plans spiralling off the edge of the historical city between the parklands of the Villa Borghese and Villa Ada to the north, around the Piazza Bologna and in the area of San Lorenzo, between the two railway stations. While the Aurelian Wall shaped the Rome of 1873 and 1883, twentieth-century Rome entered a state of pure overflow. Networks of interconnected thoroughfares blow Rome's western edge out beyond the Villa Doria Pamphili, as its eastern borders went beyond the neighbourhood of San Lorenzo, both envisaging private and undeveloped land as extensive urban parks. It took three decades and the advent of the motor car, but the historical centre of Rome was quickly enough surrounded.

The big winner in much of this was the Turinese

**Figure 5.2:** General Regulatory Plan of Rome, 1883.

property development company Società Generale Immobiliare, which acquired undeveloped and unprotected land within the city's historical borders as well as substantial swathes of its pastoral periphery. As the footprint of Rome continued to expand into the twentieth century, and especially after the Second World War, the Società earned an unenviable reputation for cynical acquisitions and low-quality residential building projects. A campaign against its practices earned its development record the rather telling moniker of the 'sack of Rome'.[3] It built for the wealthy as well as for the poor, from 1885 onwards turning the lands of the Villa Ludovisi into the well-heeled blocks flanking via Vittorio Veneto. It had a financial interest in Washington's Watergate Hotel, designed by the Roman architect Luigi Moretti, as well as in the controversial hilltop development of the Cavalieri Hilton on the Monte Mario. That the Vatican maintained a significant shareholding in the Società as it wreaked what many regarded as the worst of its damage on Rome was seen as evidence of an entirely different, capitalistically motivated set of values projected upon the city by the Church.

## The Roman Question

The art collections of the Vatican Museums are among the most impressive in the world, drawing millions of patrons through their doors each year to see Michelangelo's frescos in the chapel of Sixtus

IV (3) and those by Raphael and his disciples in the apartments of Julius II. It takes an early start indeed to secure a spot towards the front of the queue into the museums, which would allow the chance – with a little forward planning and a bit of pace – to experience these rooms, for some minutes at least, without the crowds with which they are inevitably filled. But to enjoy them requires the investment of quite some time standing alongside the now mute Leonine Wall. Beyond its tufa sit the Apostolic Palace and St Peter's Basilica as well as the Vatican grounds, in which deer used to roam. For more than half a century, though, from Rome's incorporation into a unified Italy until 1929, this ninth-century structure was a visible symbol of the dislocation of the Roman Curia from Rome itself.

The three pacts signed that year at the Lateran Palace, together comprising the Lateran Treaty, secured a reconciliation between the Kingdom of Italy and the Holy See, granting the Vatican City sovereignty as a nation within a city and describing the extent of the new Vatican City, as well as securing a degree of restitution over the losses sustained by the Church through the absorption of the Papal States into Italy. A number of major churches and palaces were rendered extra-territorial properties of the Holy See, including the major basilicas of St John Lateran (40), Santa Maria Maggiore (37) and San Paolo fuori le mura – exempt from tax and, for all practical purposes, as immune from Italian sovereignty as any foreign embassy. This

treaty between Italy and the Holy See offered a resolution to the Roman Question while securing the
formal support of the Church for the fascist regime
led by Prime Minister Benito Mussolini. Importantly,
it paved the way for Rome as the capital of an Italian
Kingdom to make a powerful claim upon St Peter's
Basilica as its symbolic and spiritual centre.

When the architect Gianlorenzo Bernini conceived
of the oval piazza that sits before the basilica during the
reign of Alexander VII, his scheme served as a study
in contrasts. One would emerge from the densely
packed streets of the Borgo into a light expanse, perfectly framing Michelangelo's dome, which had been
completed less than a century earlier. While the piazza
itself had been completed in 1667, the question of
how to approach and enter this vast public space was
one that remained poorly reconciled until the resolution of the Roman Question. The islands of buildings lining the streets of the Borgo Nuovo and Borgo
Vecchio in Nolli's eighteenth-century *Pianta Grande di
Roma* were still there, unchanged, in the 1909 plan.
It took the gumption of the 1930s and a proposal by
Marcello Piacentini – arguably Mussolini's answer to
Albert Speer – to carve out a monumental axis leading
from Hadrian's Mausoleum to the gates of St Peter's
Square and to render in stone a version of Bernini's
grand intentions for the approach to the basilica.
Without knowing better, it is easy to regard via della
Conciliazione (5) as one of the city's most natural
monumental axes, a triumph of baroque staging –

which, in many respects, it certainly is. It is, however, like a great deal of Rome's apparently historical fabric, a much more recent intervention. It is also another significant instance of the erasure of older layers of the city's buildings that were long held to have kept Rome's glorious classical past at arm's length from its auspicious 'rebirth' – in the mould of an antiquity mediated either by the Church, or by the ideologues of fascism. Built up piecemeal and in concert with the rising prominence of the Christian world and its holy sites, the dense and disordered Borgo had already been tidied and rationalized by successive popes of the fifteenth, sixteenth and seventeenth centuries. With the installation of Piacentini's monumental vista, though, making a direct connection between the ancient and modern worlds as the dual authority for Rome's place in the centre of the modern age, it was wiped clean. The scale of the project's overwriting of the old buildings of the Borgo is by no means an indictment on the fascist era alone. The twentieth-century phase of this project started in the middle of the 1930s, only to be interrupted by the Second World War; the damage done, it was completed as late as 1950 as one of the major achievements of a post-war Italy rebuilding itself and its reputation – and as such belongs to a number of projects that extended the totalizing visions of fascism into the vocabulary and ambitions of the Italian Republic. Again: continuity in rupture.

## Romanità

The distillation of ancient Rome into a set of defining morals and models has for many centuries served those who would rule the city. Augustus put Rome's image to work in this way, as did Gregory the Great, Innocent III, Julius II and Napoleon. When, in the 1920s and 1930s, Mussolini set about to place Rome under the symbol of the eagle and fasces, he did so to unify a new nation under a compelling shared language, visual style and cultural patrimony – with a carefully curated version of the monuments and fabric of Rome at its centre as part of a broad cultural programme recalling the city's natural predisposition to imperial rule and the greatness and grandeur firmly embedded in its basic makeup. At the heart of this image was an imperial Rome: a precedent for his own efforts to bed down and extend a diminutive Italian Empire that had edged its way in as a late and minor player in the land-grab for Africa. Its moral authority, though, was the city of Rome, its longevity, grandeur and permanence amplified through the isolation, as beacons, of those ancient monuments that had made it as far as the twentieth century as part of any number of the ancient layers of Rome's complex historical fabric. Put simply, very few of the ancient monuments we might admire today ever enjoyed the isolation they now possess as islands of antiquity in an otherwise modern city before they were granted that clarity with the swing of the wrecking ball.

The innate 'Romanness', or *romanità*, claimed for these fragments was secured by forcing a rhetorical distance between those monuments and the everyday life with which they were surrounded. In this rhetoric resided the authority of historical inevitability. The Theatre of Marcellus (35) had, for instance, been obscured by century upon century's worth of accretions: shops and apartments. But in an eviction, excavation and restoration project spanning from 1926 to 1932, it was stripped of its dishevelment and made to stand in the Roman landscape as a recollection of the age of the emperors. The 'recovery' of the Augusteum (10) and the staging to which it was subject at the hands of architect Vittorio Ballio Morpurgo over the course of the 1930s, ahead of the Augustan bimillennial, is another instance of this historical sanitization. The greatest moments in the city's history stand apart from the city itself – a matter of destiny.

Perhaps the most troubling monument to these ambitions, though, remains the controversial via dell'Impero, now called via dei Fori Imperiali, which was opened in 1932 after construction commenced the year following the dictator's 1922 March on Rome. It cuts violently through the so-called imperial forums that expanded beyond the original Forum Romanum through the efforts of Julius Caesar and various of his successors, including Augustus himself, Vespasian (Temple of Peace), Domitian (Forum of Nerva) and Trajan. It presents a study in contrasts: the Colosseum, a privileged, singular structure clearly signalling a debt of the Italian Kingdom to its imperial antecedent, while the imperial forums, many of which had fallen into a state of disrepair, less highly regarded than their predecessor, were somehow up for grabs. A scene in Fellini's 1972 film *Roma* comes to mind: tunnellers laying the path of the city's post-war metro lines break through a wall into an ancient chamber covered in frescos, which swiftly disappear as they are exposed to the modern air. On via dell'Impero the disappearance of antiquities was less an accident than collateral loss. There were too many artefacts that were too expensive to catalogue, and the problem they posed too difficult to resolve in light of the pressing need to clarify the symbolic straight line separating the Altare della Patria (the Vittoriano, 36) – a gaudy nineteenth-century design completed in 1925 – from the Colosseum. Buildings of all kinds had grown along that route over the many centuries separating Mussolini from Maxentius. It was difficult to distinguish these monuments from the more than 5,500 medieval and modern dwellings in the way, so they had to go.

## *Open City*

Standing on the steps of the Vittoriano, looking down via del Corso with the ancient city centre to your back and the thirteenth-century BC Flaminio Obelisk in the distance, you can share the view enjoyed by Adolf Hitler, Benito Mussolini and their senior staff on the occasion of the Führer's visit to the Italian capital in May 1938. The confidence and vision they shared diminished in the years that followed, and as the Second World War drew to a close in 1945, Roberto Rossellini's film *Roma, città aperta* (*Rome, Open City*) exposed the German occupation of Rome to a glaringly harsh light, offering in a neo-realist register a document of the basic transformation to which Italy's allegiances had been subject in the difficult intervening years.

Italy had entered the European war as one of the Axis Powers – a natural fulfilment of Mussolini's ideological proximity to German Nazism and their shared commitment to a fascist future. However, facing the realities of its prospects after a difficult African campaign, the Allied landing in Sicily and aggressive bombardment of its towns and cities, Italy threw its hat in with the Allied Forces as a cobelligerent in 1943 and rendered Rome a target of German aggression. The term 'open city' refers to the decision not to defend Rome against occupation, thereby preserving its fabric and its people (goes the logic) from unnecessary destruction – the model set by Paris in 1940 – and on Italy's surrender to the Anglo-American Allies, German forces quickly occupied the Italian capital. The Villa Massimo – since 1905 the German Academy, a function it again serves – became the headquarters of the Waffen-SS, and as Rossellini masterfully captures in film, the city was subject to German administration.

Rome suffered at the hands of both sides. Pius XII had asked the American president Franklin D. Roosevelt to spare Rome's ancient cultural landscape from damage as it sustained intensely destructive air raids from British and American bombers seeking to disable the city's airfields and rail yards. But thousands were killed and injured in 1943 and 1944 and, despite its neutrality and cultural importance to both sides, even the Vatican City was hit by British bombs.

Two contemporary sites, both at some physical distance from the Vatican, describe something of Rome's experience of the Second World War and the German occupation. The quarter of San Lorenzo is now dominated by the fascist-era campus of La Sapienza, Rome's first university, historically located in the area around the modern *rione* of Sant'Eustacchio (10). As San Lorenzo borders the adjacent neighbourhood of Tiburtina, however, and you move from a fabric of apartments to the funerary landscape of Campo Verano, you encounter the sixth-century Basilica of San Lorenzo fuori le mura. (It would be as easy to take the newly amplified high-speed rail train station at Tiburtina as a starting point and make your way to this church through the cemetery, which serves as a reminder that as late as the nineteenth century, when Giuseppe Valadier laid out these grounds for burial, this part of the contemporary city was literally beyond the walls.) The significance of the site dates to the third century and the martyrdom of St Lawrence in AD 258, within a century of which Constantine had built a small oratory where the reconstructed church now stands.

The proximity of San Lorenzo to the rail yards that

share its name, however, placed it directly in harm's way, and a hit to the façade of this ancient basilica during a US Air Force assault on the city on 19 July 1943 rendered it a symbolic casualty among 1,800 lives lost on that day. The damage to this venerable building provided a popular focus for those suffering from the destruction of the largely working-class neighbourhoods of San Lorenzo and its surrounds, prompting the pontiff that very afternoon to visit the patriarchal basilica in the aftermath of the bombing and to distribute relief funds to Rome's beleaguered citizens. Today it is hard to imagine the damage done to the area of San Lorenzo and its environs. The basilica is restored and the violence has been consigned to history – a relatively recent episode, remembered by many, but only one among the many sustained by Rome over centuries.

Another monument from these years requires a trip outside the city, some distance down via Appia Antica, and a detour between the catacombs of the canonized third-century Pope Callixtus I (San Callisto) and the martyred St Sebastian (San Sebastiano) – a victim of Diocletian's persecutions of Christians. During the height of the German occupation of Rome, partisan forces mounted an attack on the German Bozen police regiment, costing it thirty-two of its number, which triggered a disproportionate reprisal that saw 335 prisoners executed at the Ardeatine caves where (today) via Ardeatine meets via delle Sette Chiese. This chapter in the city's wartime history is memorialized in a Monument to the Martyrs designed by the architects Giuseppe Perugini and Mario Fiorentini and sculptor Mirko Basaldella – a transformation of the caverns themselves (where the bodies were discovered) into a national shrine. Outside, a massive floating concrete structure hovers over the graves of the victims like 'a closing tomb', to recall Terry Kirk's expression.[4] Sunlight creeps in around the edges of the monument as if it is about to disappear, and the ceiling surface weighs down on the space with the insistence of a troubled conscience.

Thus Rome's two-speed experience of the Second World War: as something recent and profound that sits heavily and shapes the past, an exceptional event within the passage of time; and as something quickly assimilated and neutralized, like so much else, as memory fades and history, as always, piles up.

## From the Foro Mussolini to the XVII Olympiad

Mussolini had reconceived Mazzini's Third Rome: no longer a Rome for the people, it was the Rome of Fascist Man. As we have already seen, nothing was off limits in his instrumentalization of the city to meet the ideological needs of Italian fascism. History was rewritten, the populace reorganized. Dissenters were treated much the same way as the clutter around Rome's ancient monuments. To Rome were added entirely new quarters informed by the values of Mussolini's creed. In the north of the city, across the Tiber from the neighbourhood of Flaminio, an advanced institute was established for training teachers in physical education, fostering the muscular values of the well-honed body: disciplined, capable, elegant. Dating to 1928, the original structure still stands, but was quickly joined by a triumphal sporting complex called the Stadio dei Marmi (figure 5.3) – its athletics track lined with idealized, depictions of Fascist Man rendered in Carrara marble – and a large sporting arena, the Stadio dei Cipressi (later the Stadio di Centomila, reflecting its 100,000 capacity), which was not completed until after the Second World War, and was renamed ahead of the 1960 Olympics as the Stadio Olimpico. While the complex as a whole grew piecemeal from its original intentions over the course of a decade, it came to be called the

**Figure 5.3:** The Stadio dei Marmi, Foro Italico, 1960.

Foro Mussolini (later the Foro Italico) – a name set in stone, as it were, when an enormous obelisk (also in white Carrara marble) was raised with Mussolini's own name blazoned down its length, MVSSOLINI DVX, the only public monument to the dictator still standing in the aftermath of his defeat.

That said, the district known as E42 also speaks volumes with regard to the ambitions of the fascist regime. Mussolini planned work towards the Esposizione Universale Roma, the EUR, which Rome was to have hosted beyond the city's southern suburbs in 1942. It is now a thriving middle-class neighbourhood, unlike almost any other neighbourhood in the city owing to the ceremonial scale of its streets. Until the outbreak of war, it was intended to host the world in a celebration of two decades of Italian cultural achievement. For many, its monuments have undergone the transition from derision to regard, and the legacies of some of Italy's finest modern architects have been whitewashed of their original associations. The best-known landmark of the structures realized for this event is commonly, and significantly, called the Square Colosseum – the Palazzo della Civiltà Italiana (the Palace of Italian Civilization, or, more tellingly, Civiltà del Lavoro, Civilization of Labour) – and it sits on an axis perpendicular to the more ceremonial axis running south towards the major sports arena. It was completed mid-way through the war, marking the end of an era rather more than its triumphs. Many of the projects interrupted by the war were completed much later, as in the Palazzo dei Congressi (figure 5.4), which Adalberto Libera commenced in 1938, but only finished in 1954 – a bridge from his rationalist past and discomfiting proximity to reactionary ideas to a democratic, humanist future. (The Palazzo dei Congressi may be his best-known Roman project, but his most famous work is arguably the Casa Malaparte, immortalized by Jean-Luc Godard and Brigitte Bardot in the 1963 film *Le Mépris* [*Contempt*].)

Another monument to this transition is the city's major railway station, Termini. In its original form, it had been designed by Salvatore Bianchi in the 1860s – one of the favoured architects, wrote Manfredo Tafuri, of the Roman patriciate.[5] It was initiated under the

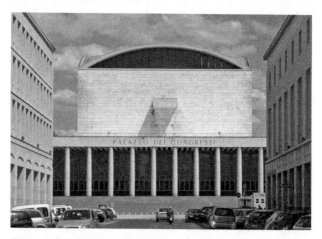

**Figure 5.4:** Palazzo dei Congressi, EUR, by Adalberto Libera (1938–54).

pope and completed under the king, spanning one regime change; and in its replacement it would span another. Bianchi's station had been intended to serve as a central station for Rome as it was rather than Rome as it would soon be, and as early as the 1920s it had become obsolete for the needs of this twentieth-century city. The first scheme to modernize the station was conceived as part of the public works programme initiated ahead of the universal exposition of 1942. The task was entrusted to the architect Angiolo Mazzoni, to whom many public buildings and amenities of Mussolini's regime owe their design. It was a study in the relationship between the historical rhythms of the archway and the clean lines of architectural modernism – a discussion, in its composition, between tradition and the past, on the one hand, and progress, on the other. As an amenity, rail travel spoke to the latter, and as one gateway to the grand celebration of Rome's progress under Mussolini's rule, the brief for Termini was to express Italy's technological advancement with a Roman language. The arched windows adorning its travertine arcades are perfectly legible along the lengths of via Giovanni Giolitti and via Marsala, which flank the tracks, with the rhythm of the arches giving way to a modern composition of the windows and openings along its length. The arches speak to those of the Palazzo della Civiltà Italiana at the EUR – a product of the same time and shared values.

Those values were explicitly supplanted by the

new building conceived shortly after the end of the war and completed in 1950 to the design of Eugenio Montuori, Leo Calini and Annibale Vitellozzi. While Mazzoni had housed the various functions of the railway station down the flanks of this complex, the new architects collaborating on this site realized a terminus building, running across the front of what is now the Piazza del Cinquecento, into which those functions were relocated. It was light, open, functional and fluid: an expression in architecture, many observed, of the new values of Italian democracy.[6]

More than two decades after E42 faltered, the staging of Rome for a newly established democratic republic similarly demanded much of one of its most important events: invoking antiquity to fresh, if familiar, ends; and rhetorically setting aside the city's recent ignominious involvement with reactionary politics. Many of the events of the XVII Olympiad of 1960 were held in purpose-built, highly modern structures engineered by Pier Luigi Nervi, such as the Palazzetto dello Sport, which gave impetus to complete the EUR across the 1950s. Nervi collaborated with Libera in the design of 1,350 new apartments for the Olympic Village (east of via Flaminia, in the blocks north of what is now the Parco della Musica), which were absorbed into the city in the wake of the Games. His facilities on via Flaminia included a smaller Palazzetto dello Sport on the Piazza Apollodoro – a low basketball dome, designed in collaboration with Vitellozzi – and his elegant Corso di

Francia, running through the village, illustrates the city's new infrastructural works built to make Rome a better host to the Games. Other events returned to the Foro Italico – in part sustaining their association with the fascist regime and in part attempting to redeem the nation by sanitizing the artefacts of its failed ambitions. A new swimming complex and a completed Stadio Olimpico consolidated the sporting facilities on this site. Centred on Flaminio and the Foro Italico in Rome's north, and the EUR to the south, the Games offered a chance to present a new, open Rome, democratic and modern.

It was not all about the recent past, though. Several events recalled the historical importance of the Games for Roman antiquity. Gymnastics events were, for instance, staged in the Baths of Caracalla. Wrestling matches were held in the colossal Basilica Nova (38) on the Forum Romanum. And the marathon took competitors along via Appia Antica before a triumphal finish through the Arch of Constantine (39).

In the staging of the 1960 Olympic Games, Rome processed the legacy of the interwar years. The city's antiquity was no longer the source of its supremacy in the contemporary world – a natural right to rule – but a glue binding this present moment to a deep and continuous history, a source of pride in a period of recovery and an opportunity to accelerate the development of much-needed urban infrastructure to allow the city to serve a modern nation. This moment was not without its problems, of course. The vacancy left by fascism had been filled by a Christian Democratic mayoralty under Salvatore Rebecchini that had, in the eyes of many, turned the city wholesale over to a corrupt and aggressive development – that same development that had broken past the city's nineteenth-century boundaries and supported the indiscriminate population growth of the periphery. For these critics, the 1960 Games stood for political cynicism and warranted distrust.

## Housing the Romans

At the end of the Second World War, Rome faced a significant period of repair: literally, in the wake of Allied aggression and German occupation; and figuratively, in a social realignment from the political right to the centre and centre-left. Internal migration saw highly accelerated rates of urbanization in the 1940s and 1950s and a concomitant need for the large industrial and administrative Italian cities to provide for rapidly growing populations. Rome was no different from anywhere else in having to negotiate the legacy of its 1920s and 1930s, the omnipresence of an Americanized consumer culture, the spectre of corruption and organized crime, and political instability. The city that became the Italian capital in 1871 had a population numbering barely more than 200,000 people. This Rome was comfortably accommodated by its walls, which no longer offered defence, but continued to define the city as such. By the end of the

1940s, however, there were eight times that number: 1.6 million Romans crammed into an inadequate stock of housing and the existing infrastructure simply could not cope. That number increased by more than half a million more across the 1950s, and by as much again over the 1960s.

A programme that did more than almost any other entity to address this crisis was the INA-Casa, a housing initiative by the Istituto Nazionale delle Assicurazione, the national insurance agency, which with government support began in 1949 to build working-class dwellings. The scale of the project meant that construction occurred on the outskirts of the city – on undeveloped sites in the suburban periphery. The regulatory plan of 1931 had predicted a degree of expansion into the periphery, and had importantly predicated some of the infrastructure on which the housing accommodating the post-war population explosion would rely. Taking the Metro 'linea A' towards Anagnina (perhaps heading for the bus to take you to Ciampino), the stop for San Giovanni indicates the moment when you pass through the Aurelian Wall and the edge, therefore, of Rome's historical limits. From Porta Furba-Quadraro onwards, the Metro follows the path of the medieval via Tuscolana, and if you were to exit at any of the four stops from Numidio Quadrato to Subaugusta you would be in easy walking distance of one of the INA-Casa's most significant developments.

Tuscolano was developed in three stages across the 1950s, with different design teams at different stages working with different building types on different sites within the overall 35-hectare complex. (The area of the Vatican City state is not much larger than this, at 44 hectares.) INA-Casa built 3,150 units housing 18,000 people, give or take, in buildings that range in scale from free-standing family homes to row houses to ten-storey towers: two million square metres of floor area. There were village amenities intended to foster a community spirit: a church, markets, community centre, and so forth, but like much of Rome at this moment, there were no parks to speak of.[7] Spread in the blocks between via del Quadraro and via Valerio Publicola, south of via Tuscolana, Stage I had been built quickly to the design of more than a dozen architects, and the variety of designers is reflected in the heterogeneity of the appearance of the towers themselves. Spreading west of via del Quadraro, Tuscolano II spanned the full decade of the 1950s. A team led by Saverio Muratori and Mario de Renzi worked up a series of standardized apartments, including the 'boomerangs' that run south from the imposing block that dominates the Largo Spartaco. Earning the greatest critical acclaim, Adalberto Libera developed the design of the third part of the project (1950–4) on the block between Tuscolano II and the railway line, designing a much smaller number of units conceived as single-level apartments arranged around courtyards – his *Unità orizzontale*, or horizontal units – and a single four-floor block with apartments. Together housing fewer than a thousand of the residents of Tuscolano, it nonetheless experimented with the lessons learned from those architects and builders housing large numbers of people in close range in such warmer climes as northern Africa – one of the more celebrated examples of post-war housing design addressing this problem, and a strong example of the modern transfer of architectural models and strategies into the modern Italian city from elsewhere in the Mediterranean.

Spread around the edges of the formal Tuscolano complex, various private developers capitalized on the new roads and amenities that had been brought to the neighbourhood by INA-Casa and further developed the blocks and blocks of cookie-cutter apartment buildings – sometimes changing form from one block to the next, reflecting a fresh developer and a fresh set of eyes on the problem of balancing land use, construction costs and profit. In the opening scene of Francesco Rosi's 1963 film *Le mani sulla città* (*Hands over the City*), a Neapolitan developer holds forth at the edges of *his* city, new apartments visible in the middle distance, on the 'gold of today', that land zoned for farming but perfect for building upon so long as the city could be persuaded to shift the direction of its planned growth and provide the hook-ups to ensure water-supply, roads, sewerage and the various other amenities needed to support new neighbourhoods. A montage of anonymous apartment towers follows to the first salvo of a punchy Piero Piccioni score. For many, especially on the left, Rosi's dramatization of the crimes of opportunity perpetrated against Naples on its periphery resonated with the experience of most if not all of the cities of modern Italy – and certainly with that of Rome.

## I grandi progetti

The term *grands projets* invokes Paris in the era of François Mitterrand, whose new national library building – Dominique Perrault's four translucent towers – brought this phase of massive public works to a dramatic end in 1998. In Rome, though, the *grandi progetti* of Francesco Rutelli were only just entering their stride at this time. His progressive mayoralty spanned 1993 to 2001, and left three monumental legacies in Rome's cultural landscape. Rome had barely seen an intervention in the city's historical fabric in the years leading up to his tenure, with decades of shoring up roads and service infrastructure and constructing housing, schools and other buildings needed by an ever-growing populace. One index of the slow pace of development is the city mosque built for Rome on the western edge of the expansive park of the Villa Ada, at the tip of Parioli in the city's north. Designed by Roman architect Paolo Portoghesi in collaboration with Sami Mousawi and Vittorio Gigliotti, the project took two decades from inception to completion (1974–95). It proved a success among critics, if not universally, and especially so as architectural postmodernism has returned to a state of grace. But it demonstrated, too, the ponderous pace at which significant new public institutions were built, even under relatively favourable conditions.

On the other side of Parioli, on the eastern flank of Flaminio (close to both the Stadio Flaminio and the Palazzetto dello Sport), the Parco della Musica speaks to a changed pace – in a sense. The possibility of a major municipal music venue had been mooted for decades, since at least the 1930s. Its main beneficiary would be the sixteenth-century Accademia Nazionale di Santa Cecilia – and classical music in general. An initiative to bring these plans to fruition was launched in 1993 and the workshop of Genovese architect Renzo Piano was commissioned to build a vast 'music park' on undeveloped lands at the base of the area hitherto shaped by the building works of the 1960 Olympic Games. It was completed at a snappy pace, opened in 2002 after a mere eight years of works. Its centrepiece buildings are three auditoriums, arranged around an open-air theatre, that recall the shallow curves of the pines that fill Rome with abundance. Although the project's intentions did not survive intact – a previously unknown pre-Roman village was discovered in the excavation phase – in its final form it served two important functions. For one thing, it ushered in a phase of public building that deferred to the fame of the 'starchitect' to ensure forward momentum towards completion and the attention of an audience spanning from architects themselves to the popular media. As a starchitect, Piano may be less stellar than others with a claim to the epithet, but he even now stands as perhaps the best-known living Italian architect – and the prominence of his cultural architecture, from the Centre Pompidou in Paris to the Jean-Marie Tjibaou Cultural Centre in Noumea, secured critical attention for the Roman project. For another, and more importantly, it signalled the reinvigoration of Flaminio as a zone of cultural investment.

When the Parco della Musica opened, the process to build a new museum of contemporary art (MAXXI) on another Flaminio site had already resulted in a commission for the British firm of Zaha Hadid Architects. The project outlived Rutelli's mayoralty, being finished in 2009, but it nevertheless shared the same broader outlook and urgency that had ensured the successful completion of the complex by Piano, a short walk along the street that becomes via Guido Reni. A museum dedicated to the broad spectrum of the arts – from conceptual practices to artful engineering – of the late twentieth and twenty-first centuries, it was the subject of a hotly contested competition that attracted proposals from a number of the most significant architects of its moment. Hadid's scheme worked with the theme of fluidity in defining the form of both the building, as a work of architecture, and the institution, as a setting in which to process contemporary art as it enters history. It is, in many respects, an open work in which internal and exterior zones are defined through the use of subtle borders, and in this it resembles something of the problem of Rome at its own edges. Escaping the archaeological complications discovered on the site of the Parco della Musica, MAXXI was not obliged to confront a history of any great antiquity – even if the design of the museum responds to the industrial history of its own site. Rome registers here as an institutional abstraction in which the burdens of history are largely absent. These are more a problem for the historical centre.

This cannot be said for the most controversial of the projects initiated during Rutelli's tenure in the Palazzo Senatorio. We encountered Richard Meier's building for the Augustan Ara Pacis (9) in Chapter 1: a building initiated through the direct intervention of the Mayor of Rome to return the Augustan monument to a standing proper to its historical importance. Whereas the large new works by Hadid and Piano sat beyond the historical centre of Rome, the Ara Pacis was in the midst of the battleground: surrounding a work of great antiquity and fronting off the fascist-era structures that sought to tame the Augustan legacy, reconciling it with the prevailing ideology of the 1930s. The project was seen to its conclusion by Rutelli's successor, Walter Veltroni. When Veltroni, in turn, left the mayoralty in 2008 to pursue national office, his reactionary successor vowed within his first week to demolish the building. But it survived Gianni Alemanno to fight another day, in doing so securing a small part for itself among the layers of the history of Rome. Under the plane of its roof, the Augustan monument connects the visitor to one of the most celebrated chapters in this city's rich history – Rome at the centre of a global empire – and always the idea on which it rests: the intrepid Aeneas, edging towards his destiny as father of the Romans; and Romulus, whose plough, they say, was responsible for making it all happen.

# Selected Sources

The literature on Rome is vast, and to write a book of this scale is to engage in a contest between knowledge and narrative. The gaps in this work are, necessarily, many and will frustrate the specialist in any aspect of the long and complex history of this city and its various institutions. As a book intended to introduce and orientate, however, it also needs to direct the avid reader to the next tier of sources with which to pursue a fuller and more complex encounter with the literature of Rome than can be had with walking this city's streets literally or figuratively armed with these pages alone. A bibliography to fully service even a short history of Rome would quickly exceed the pages allocated to this book as a whole, and it would not be an exaggeration to call it a lifetime of reading. The articles and books that follow, then, have been more important than others in shaping my own attempt at writing a short history of Rome. Some of the sources are overtly generalist and others clearly specialist. The risk is that they reveal too much about my own prejudices and preoccupations, but what follows is as good a place to start going further as any other.

I have found it important to read the history of Rome through its architectural and urban history and through the tangible artefacts of its art. To that extent, although it offers a rather dense and technical guide to the art and monuments of Rome, there is nothing that surpasses the blocky red Touring Club Italiano's *Guida d'Italia: Roma*. I have the 10th edition (Milan, 2008), but it has been in press since 1925. Its maps are excellent and its details precise, and even though it is published in Italian, its clear identification of works, their artists and their dates can be a great help to a reader unfamiliar with the language. As a practical aid, I have had Maps 2.0 open on my iMac while working these pages up – more than a little of this writing was done closer to the Pacific than the Tiber – and am continually impressed with the quality of its renders.

As general sources, Christopher Hibbert's *Rome: The Biography of a City* (London: Penguin, 1987) and Robert Hughes's *Rome* (London: Weidenfeld & Nicolson, 2011) offer excellent insights while being at once both highly personalized and organized around art historical categories, which I have sought, against my inclinations, to set aside as much as I could. The multi-volume reference work *Storia dell'architettura italiana* (published by the Milanese press Electa since 1997) offers a conspectus of developments in Roman architecture and planning over many centuries while offering critico-historical essays that draw contemporary scholarship into the analysis. The edited volumes of Laterza's *Storia di Roma dell'antichità a oggi* (Rome, 2002– ) offer a substantial array of contemporary scholarly voices on the scope of Roman history. Alta

Macadam and Annabel Barber's *Blue Guide* covering *Rome and Its Environs* (1974; Taunton: Somerset Books, 10th edn, 2010) has been to hand throughout, and numerous other guidebooks of varying vintages have confirmed some of my habits and upset others.

Several modern essays have treated the subject of this city as a lens through which to regard other matters and I considered three of these in my Introduction: Georg Simmel's essay 'Rome', reproduced in English (by Ulrich Teuchner and Thomas M. Kemple) in *Theory, Culture & Society* (24, nos 7–8 [2007], 30–7), but originally published as 'Rom: Ein ästhetische Analyse' (in *Die Zeit* 191 [1898], 137–9). I first encountered Simmel's essay by reading Bart Verschaffel's *Rome/Over Theatraliteit* (Ghent: Vlees en Beton, 1996), which is itself a fascinating and too little known portrait of the city. Simmel's 'Rome' is one of his three 'Italian' essays that consider Florence, Rome and Venice in turn, and which have been gathered into a single volume in German (and Spanish) and into the aforementioned issue of *Theory, Culture & Society*. Freud's reflections on Rome have been widely celebrated, and can be found in the *Standard Edition* (all by The Hogarth Press and the Institute of Psychoanalysis, London, edited by James Strachey). I have referred to later, discrete editions of *The Interpretation of Dreams* (London: Allen & Unwin, 1955) and *Civilization and Its Discontents* (London: The Hogarth Press and the Institute of Psychoanalysis, 1973). The piece on which the Introduction concludes, *Storia della mia morte*, I was first shown to me by my wife in a collection of miscellaneous short stories while on holiday – perhaps in a *Reader's Digest* or the like – but the image has never left me. The definitive English translation is by Ruth Draper as Lauro de Bosis, *The Story of My Death* (Oxford: Oxford University Press, 1933). Beyond these, I have found Pier Vittorio Aureli's *The Possibility of an Absolute Architecture* (Cambridge, Mass.: MIT Press, 2011) a useful provocation.

I have relied on Christopher Smith's expertise in the ancient history of Rome and his command of the historiographical terrain. I highly recommend his book *The Etruscans: A Very Short Introduction* (Oxford: Oxford University Press, 2014) – alongside two other volumes from this series: David M. Gwynn, *The Roman Republic*; and Christopher Kelly, *The Roman Empire* (Oxford: Oxford University Press, both 2012). Smith's contribution to *Mediterranean Urbanization 800–600 BC*, edited by Robin Osborne and Barry Cunliffe (Oxford: Oxford University Press, 2005) – 'The Beginnings of Urbanization in Rome' – has been instructive, as has his earlier book *Early Rome and Latium: Economy and Society c. 1000 to 500 BC* (Oxford: Clarendon Press, 1996). At the other end of the spectrum is the work of Andrea Carandini, published in English for a broader audience as *Rome: Day One*, trans. Stephen Sartarelli (Princeton, NJ: Princeton University Press, 2011) – readers will doubtless find this exciting, even as his work quickly divides his readers. (His studies of the so-called Romulean Wall first appeared as 'Le mura del Palatino. Nuova fonte sulla Roma di età Regia', *Bollettino di archaeologia* 16–18 [1992], 1–18.)

David Watkin's *The Roman Forum* (London: Profile, 2009) is an impassioned and erudite account of that key site, and while it takes some issue with *Rome: An Oxford Archaeological Guide*, by Amanda Claridge (Oxford: Oxford University Press, 1998; 2nd edn, 2010), and with what he casts as an archaeological worldview, they can be read alongside one another to appreciate the give and take between fact and narrative with which both are engaged. More broadly, on Rome's ancient and early Christian monuments, Claridge's *Guide* is both excellent and indispensable. On the legends around the life and death of Romulus and Remus, I have learned much from T. P. Wiseman's *Remus: A Roman Myth* (Cambridge: Cambridge University Press, 1995) – while it has its detractors, it signals clearly enough when it is exploring an idea and when it rests solidly on a bed of scholarship to offer a significant source on the republican construction of Roman identity. See also Jesse Benedict Carter, 'The Death of Romulus', *American Journal of Archaeology* 13, no. 1 (1909), 19–29; Andreas Mehl, *Roman Historiography* (Malden, Mass.: Wiley-Blackwell, 2011); and Gerald P. Verbrugghe, 'Fabius Pictor's "Romulus and Remus"', *Historia: Zeitschrift für Alte Geschichte* 30, no. 2 (1981), 236–8. On early Roman historiography and the role of history in development of the Romulus–Remus myth, see Marion Dittman,

'The Development of Historiography among the Romans', *Classical Journal* 30, no. 5 (1935), 287–96.

A pair of historical articles have spurred me along at key moments – both thoroughly superseded by later scholarship but nonetheless evocative of one image of historical Rome as a city in change: Jesse Benedict Carter (again), 'The Evolution of the City of Rome from Its Origin to the Gallic Catastrophe', *Proceedings of the American Philosophical Society* 48, no. 192 (1909), 130–1; and Walter Dennison, 'The Roman Forum as Cicero Saw It', *Classical Journal* 3, no. 8 (1908), 318–26 – which effectively offer bookend views on Rome at the start and end of the Republic. My tour of the Servian Wall and appreciation of its pre-history has been shaped by Seth G. Bernard, 'Continuing the Debate on Rome's Earliest Circuit Walls', *Papers of the British School at Rome (PBSR)* 80 (October 2012), 1–44, which I have read alongside Droysen's map from his *Allgemeiner Historischer Handatlas* (1896) – images of which proliferate online. For some years now Robert Coates-Stephens has published annual 'Notes from Rome' in the *PBSR*, documenting new archaeological finds and significant events in the archaeology and ancient history of Rome.

The imperial history of Rome opens up a plethora of themes on which books, both specialist and accessible, abound. Overwhelmingly so. Mary Beard's *SPQR* (London: Profile, 2015) offers an excellent way to broaden knowledge of the Roman Republic and Roman Empire – a subject on which she has written a great deal. For a close reading of Rome's experience as an ancient metropolis, from its emergence as a major Mediterranean settlement to the imperial departure to Constantinople, see Stephen L. Dyson, *Rome: A Living Portrait of an Ancient City* (Baltimore, MD: Johns Hopkins University Press, 2010).

On the life of the Pantheon, I have deferred the scholarship of Tod A. Marder, especially his articles in the *Journal of the Society of Architectural Historians* (*JSAH*); but he has more recently edited, with Mark Wilson Jones, *The Pantheon: From Antiquity to Present* (Cambridge: Cambridge University Press, 2015). Students of this building will find this an excellent place to exercise their appreciation of its rich history. On the Colosseum, the volume written by Mary Beard and Keith Hopkins (Cambridge, Mass.: Harvard University Press, 2011) is an excellent introduction to that building and (or I should say *in*) its history.

I found most helpful J. Bert Lott's excellent study of the neighbourhood-level organization of religion, government and society in *The Neighborhoods of Augustan Rome* (Cambridge: Cambridge University Press, 2004). On popular culture and leisure I have consulted J. P. Toner: *Leisure and Ancient Rome* and *Popular Culture and Ancient Rome* (Cambridge: Polity, 2013 and 2009, respectively); on the history of flooding in Rome, I recommend Gregory S. Aldrete, *Floods of the Tiber in Ancient Rome* (Baltimore: Johns Hopkins University Press, 2007); on Rome's religious systems and relationships, see the two-volume study by Mary Beard, John

North and Simon Price, *Religions of Rome* (Cambridge: Cambridge University Press, 1998); as well as Jörg Rüpke's *Religion of the Romans* (Cambridge: Polity, 2007). Among the various aged Penguin paperbacks and old-school historical syntheses in my library, I have found Pierre Grimal's historiographical classic *La civilisation romaine* (Paris: Arthaud, 1960), published in English as *The Civilization of Rome* (trans. W. S. Maguinness) by Allen & Unwin (1963), to be most helpful in connecting the city to, for instance, agriculture and religion. *How to Manage Your Slaves* (London: Profile, 2014), the satirical guide by Jerry Toner (as Marcus Sidonius Falx) to the ins and outs of slavery, offered no end of insights into that aspect of the Roman world. On day-to-day life, I enjoyed Alberto Angela's *Day in the Life of Ancient Rome* (trans. Gregory Conti, New York: Europa, 2009) – a theme on which many other volumes have been written.

Ancient Rome has been subject to numerous treatments in film, television and literature – too many to recount, but easily found. I would be remiss, though, not to mention two fine novels treating key figures of Rome's imperial history: *Augustus*, by John Williams (New York: Viking, 1972); and Marguerite Yourcenar's 1951 novel *Memoirs of Hadrian* (originally *Mémoires d'Hadrien*, New York: Farrar, Straus and Giroux, 2005).

Turning to the medieval history of Rome, the magisterial and highly readable study by Richard Krautheimer – *Rome: Profile of a City, 312–1308* (Princeton, NJ:

Princeton University Press, 1980) – is hardly something to pack for a weekend away, but it offers an
engaging and highly erudite reflection on the play
between the city of Rome, its population and its institutions over a crucial and regularly overlooked millennium in Roman history. If I have followed it too closely
at times, I have also used it as a springboard to discover
the work of other writers in this field – some of whom
have offered mild corrections to his reading of specific works and counterweights to his interpretations.
Krautheimer's 1979 Una's Lectures – *Three Christian
Capitals: Topography & Politics* (Berkeley: University of
California Press, 1983) – likewise offer crucial insights
into the processes by which Rome was Christianized
in the fourth and fifth centuries and place the city in
conversation with Constantinople and Milan. Joan
Barclay-Lloyd contributed several drawings and much
research to these volumes, and for further reading on a
number of significant medieval churches I recommend
her work, which includes the articles 'The Building
History of the Medieval Church of S. Clemente in
Rome', *JSAH* 45, no. 3 (1986), 197–223; and 'Medieval
Dominican Architecture at Santa Sabina in Rome, c.
1219–c. 1320', *PBSR* 72 (2004), 231–92.

On specific aspects of the Roman middle ages,
there is a rich academic literature. Some books have
proven particularly useful in helping me to negotiate an unfamiliar terrain. On the medieval papacy and
the relationship between liturgy, architecture and the
pontifical office, I value Mary Stroll's *Symbols as Power:*

*The Papacy following the Investiture Contest* (Leiden: Brill, 1991); on the image of Rome cultivated throughout Europe, *Roma Felix: Formation and Reflections of Medieval Rome*, edited by Éamonn Ó Carrigáin and Carol Neuman de Vegvar; and for insight into the mentality of the era through a recently uncovered fresco, *Imagining the Human Condition in Medieval Rome: The Cistercian Fresco Cycle at Abbazia della Tre Fontane*, by Kristin B. Aavitsland (both Farnham: Ashgate, 2007 and 2012, respectively). To these I add Peter Partner, *The Lands of St Peter: The Papal States in the Middle Ages and the Early Renaissance* (Berkeley: University of California Press, 1972); Pierre Riché, *The Carolingians: A Family Who Forged Europe*, trans. Michael Idomir Allen (1983; Philadelphia: University of Pennsylvania Press, 1993); Herbert Schutz, *The Medieval Empire in Central Europe: Dynastic Continuity in the Post-Carolingian Frankish Realm, 900–1300* (Newcastle upon Tyne: Cambridge Scholars Publishing, 2010); and Chris Wickam, *Medieval Rome: Stability & Crisis of a City, 900–1150* (Oxford: Oxford University Press, 2015). On the immediate consequences of Rome's entry into the Carolingian age, see Caroline J. Goodson, *The Rome of Paschal I: Papal Power, Urban Renovation, Church Rebuilding and Relic Translation, 817–824* (Cambridge: Cambridge University Press, 2014). I have also noted Robert Bretano's *Rome before Avignon: A Social History of Thirteenth-Century Rome* (New York: Basic Books, 1974); and Ronald G. Musto's *Apocalypse in Rome: Cola di Rienzo and the Politics of a New Age*

(Berkeley: University of California Press, 2003). Claridge's *Rome* (see above) offers important archaeological insights on those early Christian churches long since overbuilt or enmeshed in Rome's pre-Christian religious history. And Goodson offers a valuable analysis of the medieval relationship with Roman antiquity in 'Roman Archaeology in Medieval Rome', in *Rome: Continuing Encounters between Past and Present*, ed. Dorigen Caldwell and Lesley Caldwell (Farnham: Ashgate, 2011), 17–34.

I anticipate Richard Wittman's book on heritage issues around the restoration of San Paolo fuori le mura, on which he has on occasion spoken publicly.

Older sources: Penguin in 1971 published Peter Llewellyn's *Rome in the Dark Ages* – not exactly a brief study, but nonetheless concise, especially when placed up against the multi-volume nineteenth-century survey *Geschichte der Stadt Rom in Mittelalter*, published between 1859 and 1872 by Ferdinand Gregorovius, which is now available in a four-volume German edition (Munich: Beck, 1988) and in English in several editions – my library has the edition of excerpts published by the University of Chicago Press as *Rome and Medieval Culture: Selections from History of the City of Rome in the Middle Ages* (1971). A nineteenth-century version of Benedict's *Mirabilia Urbis Romae* is freely available to download in a variety of formats.

Besides there being many important churches open to the public, on the ground one can visit the Museo Nazionale dell'Alto Medioevo (which covers the same period as Krautheimer's *Rome* – located in the neighbourhood of EUR, on viale Lincoln). This is just a short walk from another excellent historical museum concerned with the city's ancient history, the Museo della Civiltà Romana (on Piazza Giovanni Agnelli).

A number of books have informed my treatment of the early modern era – principally drawn from works that position debate on art, architecture and the city within the broader currents of politics, institutions, society and knowledge. In this, I have taken the opportunity to return to several volumes by Manfredo Tafuri, not least *Ricerca del rinascimento* (Turin: Einaudi, 1992; translated by Daniel Sherer as *Interpreting the Renaissance*, New Haven, Conn.: Yale University Press, 2006), *L'architettura dell'umanesimo* (Rome: Laterza, 1969) and *Via Giulia: Una utopia urbanistica del '500* (Rome: Aristide Staderini, 1973), with Luigi Salerno and Luigi Spezzaferro. I have learned much from Nicholas Temple's *Renovatio Urbis: Architecture, Urbanism and Ceremony in the Rome of Julius II* (London: Routledge, 2011). Lex Bosman's book on the reconstruction of St Peter's Basilica is a great introduction to the symbolic value of materials in that building – *The Power of Tradition: Spolia in the Architecture of St Peter's in the Vatican* (Hilversum: Uitgeverij Verloren, 2004). André Chastel's study on the art, culture and history of *The Sack of Rome, 1527* (trans. Beth Archer, Princeton, NJ: Princeton University Press, 1983) is invaluable and highly engaging. Giulio Carlo Argan's *Europe of the Capitals:*

*1600–1700* (Geneva: Skira, 1964) places Rome in the geo-political landscape of the European nation-states, negotiating the insights afforded by art, literature, urban planning and architecture. David Marshall's edited volume *The Site of Rome: Studies in the Art and Topography of Rome 1400–1750* (Rome: L'Erma di Bretschneider, 2014) explores the significance for Rome's institutions and public rituals of a number of historically rich sites and landscapes of great importance to the early modern city. Krautheimer's study on *The Rome of Alexander VII: 1655–1667* (Princeton, NJ: Princeton University Press, 1985) delves into the question of, as Peter Burke had it in the *London Review of Books* ('State Theatre', 22 January 1987), 'the difficulties [the popes] encountered in … combining the role of temporal and spiritual leader, king and priest'. Common to these three titles is a command of the highly significant relationship between art, institutions and historical events at work in these centuries.

Maarten Delbeke's research around the figures together instigating major ecclesiastical works by the sculptor and architect Gianlorenzo Bernini has offered a vital window on to the middle decades of the seventeenth century – see *The Art of Religion: Sforza Pallavicino and Art Theory in Bernini's Rome* (Farnham: Ashgate, 2012). As a notebook of sorts, containing hundreds of views of Rome ancient and (early) modern, the Taschen collection *Piranesi: The Complete Etchings* (edited by Luigi Ficacci; Cologne, 2000) has rarely been far from my keyboard. On Piranesi and the eighteenth-century world he inhabited, I recommend Lola Kantor-Kazovsky's *Piranesi as Interpreter of Roman Architecture and the Origins of his Intellectual World* (Florence: Leo S. Olschki, 2006) – an incredibly wide-ranging analysis on the workings of Rome's institutions, media and records as well as the intellectual context for Piranesi's own celebration of antiquity's magnificence; and *The Serpent and the Stylus*, edited by Mario Bevilacqua, Heather Hyde Minor and Fabio Barry (Ann Arbor: University of Michigan Press, 2007), which likewise prises open the institutional world of the eighteenth century and the relationship between what could be seen, depicted and circulated by way of fostering knowledge of ancient and contemporary Rome. Giuseppe Vasi's vast production is captured in an online project at the University of Oregon.

Rome's experience as a modern city is inextricably bound to the emergence of Italy as a modern nation. To that end, my treatment of its nineteenth- and twentieth-century architecture and urbanism has drawn on Terry Kirk's important two-volume study *The Architecture of Modern Italy* (New York: Princeton Architectural Press, 2005). Three closely related volumes have taken me deeper into specific lines of inquiry: Giorgio Ciucci, *Gli architetti e il fascismo. Architettura e città, 1922–44*; Manfredo Tafuri, *Storia dell'architettura italiana, 1944–85*; and Marco Biraghi and Silvia Micheli, *Storia dell'architettura italiana, 1985–2015* (Turin: Einaudi, 1989, 1986 and 2013, respectively). On the history of modern strategic planning in the city I have turned to a series of articles and reviews by Spiro Kostof (as noted in Chapter 5), whose exhibition on the subject is documented as *The Third Rome, 1870–1950: Traffic and Glory* (Berkeley, Calif.: University Art Museum, 1973).

On the twentieth-century experience of *romanità*, I have followed the work of Jan Nelis, particularly in *From Ancient to Modern: The Myth of Romanità during the Ventennio Fascista. The Written Imprint of Mussolini's Cult of the 'Third Rome'* (Turnhout: Brepols, 2011). To understand the social and political forces to which Rome has been subject in the post-war era, I recommend Paul Ginsborg's invaluable *History of Contemporary Italy 1943–1980* (London: Penguin, 1990), and its 'sequel', *Italy and Its Discontents: Family, Civil Society, State, 1980–2001* (London: Penguin, 2003). The trace of this history in Italy's public housing programmes, in which Rome is thoroughly implicated, is documented by Stephanie Zeier Pilat in *Reconstructing Italy: The Ina-Casa Neighborhoods of the Postwar Era* (Farnham: Ashgate, 2014); and on the relationship between urban and rural cultures in the twentieth-century urbanization of Italy, Michelangelo Sabatino, *Pride in Modesty: Modernist Architecture and the Vernacular Tradition in Italy* (Toronto: University of Toronto Press, 2010).

Looking, briefly, at cinematic sources for the cinematic century, a director like Federico Fellini is hard to bypass as someone who considers Rome in its expansion into a modern metropolis. The neo-realist tradition captures the city in its most disorientating moment of change, and in this the images of Rome captured, too, by Roberto Rossellini, Vittorio De Sica and Giuseppe De Sanctis have entered a modern canon against which the experience of the city is judged by visiting cinephiles. The preceding pages have evoked *La dolce vita* (1960) and *Roma* (1972) as studies, respectively, of the city at the cusp of a period of dramatic change and in its midst – change in its social and urban fabric and in its institutions (the ecclesiastical fashion parade on which *Roma* concludes is quite unforgettable). As critical as these might be of Rome's modernization, the city remains prone to romanticization, even of its sometimes violent past, and in this register the generational films *La meglio gioventù* (*The Best of Youth*) (2003) and *Romanzo criminale* (2005) are instructive. *La grande bellezza* (*The Great Beauty*) (2013) drew criticism for its apparent return to the world invoked by Fellini in 1960, but this does not adequately allow for the view it offers on the city, or for the burdens imposed by the nostalgia of its characters. In this it has much in common with Tom Rachman's novel *The Imperfectionists* (London: Quercus, 2010), set around an international newspaper based in Rome, grappling with the end of an era. And these two works reflect on Rome from the two competing perspectives that have long shaped this city's identity – inside and out, between which Rome's edges as an idea find a provisional clarity.

# Chronology

This chronology attempts a fairly even treatment of major events that one way or another position Rome as either a city or a geo-political entity anchored to the city. Few pages in this book spend time on Rome's achievements beyond the city walls, but events listed here invoke, for example, Rome's relationships with other powers and its acquisition of territories as important for the history of the city as such. Dates and events prior to the third century BC (and the first historians writing in their own time) are of variable reliability, and reflect the most common dating traditionally ascribed to them. The veracity of some things having occurred at all is questionable in the first centuries of Rome's history, and so this chronology places a degree of trust in Livy and his Augustan *Ab urbe condita* even when it is not strictly warranted.

**BC**

| | |
|---|---|
| 753 | Murder of Remus by Romulus and consequent foundation of Rome (21 April). (Romulus self-proclaimed as king 753–716.) |
| 750(52) | Abduction of Antemnates, Caeninenses, Crustumini and Sabine women during games devoted to Neptune Equester. |

752        Rome attacked successively in retaliation for the above abductions. All attacks repealed (excepting that of the Sabines) and counter-attacks mounted, resulting in an early extension of Roman lands and a period of Sabine co-rule.

752–716    During the reign of Romulus: Etruscan Fidenates attack Rome, which repeals the attack and counters with a successful attack on Fidenae. Veii follows suit and is repealed; Veientes besieged but not captured by Rome, which concludes a treaty with Veii.

716        Election of Numa Pompilius as King of Rome, first regal election by the Curate Assembly.

716–672    During the reign of Numa: Rome's religious structure takes on its own form, distinct from that of its neighbours.

673–642    Reign of Tullius Hostilius: Fidenae and Veii go to war with Rome and Alba Longa.

642–617    Reign of Ancus Marcius as Rome's fourth king.

616–579    Reign of Lucius Tarquinius Priscus, first of the Tarquin kings and fifth king of Rome.

588        Roman attack and plunder of the Latin town of Apiolae.

580        Roman war against Latium, including conquest over Aemeriola, Cameria, Corlelium, Crustumerium, Ficulae, Medullia and Norentium.

578–535    During the reign of Servius Tullius: Rome goes

to war against the Veientes and Etruscans with triumphs recorded in 571 and 567 BC.

535–534   Commencement of the reign of Lucius Tarquinius Superbus (Tarquin the Proud), seventh and final king of Rome (overthrown 509, died 496). A permanent peace between Rome and Etruria is secured at this time.

509   Superbus overthrown and the Roman Republic founded under Brutus and Publicola. Battle of Silva Arsia between royal army gathered from Veii and Tarquinii, with Rome celebrating victory on 1 March.

508   War with Etruscan city of Clusium, in which Rome was besieged and peace reached through treaty. Subsequent settlement of Etruscans in Rome purported to explain the naming of the Vicus Tuscus.

496/499/   Rome defeats the Latin League in the Battle of
493/ 489   Regillus.

494   First Secessio Plebis (Secession of the Plebs) over welfare. Tribune of the Plebs created.

471   Plebeian Council passes a law allowing plebeians to be organized into tribes, akin to the organization of the patrician class.

451,   Decemviri or Board of Ten appointed, in whose
450–449   time the Roman legal system is drafted – the Law of the Twelve Tables.

449   Second Secessio Plebis over abuses of power on behalf of the Decemviri.

390   Battle (or Siege) of Veii (alt. dates 405–396).

| | |
|---|---|
| 387 | Battle of the Allia (alt. date 390) and sack of Rome by the Gauls under Brennus, confirming the need to better defend the city and the wish to keep the Republic in Rome at all. |
| 361 | War with Ferentinum results in Rome taking the city. |
| 354 | Treaty agreed between Rome and the Samnites (see Samnite Wars below: 343–341, 326–304, 298–290). |
| 348 | Treaty agreed between Rome and Carthage (see Punic Wars below: 264–241, 218–201, 149–146). |
| 343–341 | First Samnite War, sparked by Rome's defence of the Campani in the face of Samnite aggression. First of a series of conflicts in which Rome asserted itself militarily beyond Latium. |
| 340–338 | Second Latin War, with the Latin League dissolved in favour of Roman dominance over Latium. |
| 330 | Sea port of Ostia founded. |
| 326–304 | Second (Great) Samnite War, the major outcome of which being Rome's dominance over the Italian peninsula, excepting Sicily and the Greek colonies. |
| 312 | Construction completed on the Aqua Appia (the first aqueduct) and via Appia (extending south from Rome). |
| 298–290 | Third Samnite War, in which Rome's command of Italy is confirmed. |

280–275    Pyrrhic War between a Greek consortium, the central Italian states and the Carthaginians – prompted by incursions into Italy by Pyrrhus of Epirus.

264–241    First Punic War (between Rome and Carthage), resulting in Sicilia being acquired by Rome as its first province.

218–201    Second Punic War, during which Hannibal crosses the Alps on elephants.

214–205    First Macedonian War with Greece and its allies against Philip V of Macedon (allied with Hannibal), introducing Rome to the Aegean military theatre.

200–196    Second Macedonian War, resulting in the military containment of Greece and the weakening of its regional position – now caught between Rome, Egypt and Syria.

192–188    Seleucid (Syrian) War between Rome and the Seleucid Empire (over Greece), from which Rome emerges as a regional power in the eastern Mediterranean and Asia Minor.

172–168    Third Macedonian War, in which Rome squashes an attempt to reinstate Greek power, resulting in its division into four client republics.

155        Embassy of the Three Philosophers to Rome, Carneades, Critolaus and Diogenes, representing Academic, Peripatetic and Stoic philosophical traditions: an appeal for reduced fines against Athens.

| | |
|---|---|
| 150–148 | Fourth Macedonian War, resulting in the division of Greece into the two Roman provinces of Achaea and Epirus. |
| 149–146 | Third Punic War, resulting in the siege and destruction of Carthage and Roman acquisition of Carthaginian territories. |
| 146 | Africa is made a Roman province. |
| 90–88 | War of the Allies (also called the Social War), securing Rome's dominion over Italy south of the Apennines. |
| 60 | Pompey the Great (Pompeius Magnus), Julius Caesar and Marcus Licinius Crassus form the First Triumvirate. |
| 58–51 | Gallic Wars, in which Caesar acquires significant power and means. |
| 49 | Returning from Gaul, Julius Caesar and his army cross the border into Roman Italy (the Rubicon River), effectively initiating civil war between Caesar and a faction of the Senate led by Pompey. Civil war spans 49–45. |
| 44 | Assassination of Julius Caesar in the Curia of Pompey (15 March – the 'Ides of March'). |
| 44–43 | Civil war between the Senate (led by Gaius Octavius, Marcus Antonius/Mark Antony and Marcus Aemelius Lepidus) and the 'Liberators' (led by Marcus Junius Brutus the Younger and Gaius Cassius Longinus), resulting in a tentative truce. |
| 44–42 | A second civil war with the Liberators, resulting in victory for the Triumvirate. |

44–36       Sicilian War between the Triumvirate and
            Sextus Pompey (son of Pompeius Magnus),
            won by the Triumvirate, weighted now towards
            Octavian.

31          Battle of Actium, part of the Republic's 'Final
            War', in which Mark Antony and the Ptolemaic
            Queen Cleopatra are defeated by Octavian
            and Agrippa, leading to the suicide of Antony
            and Cleopatra, and opening the path for the
            Augustan principate.

27          The so-called First Settlement, from which date
            is traditionally taken the establishment of the
            Roman Empire.

23          Second Settlement, in which Augustus resigns
            his consulship, but acquires wide-ranging
            authority over matters domestic and foreign.

17          Secular Games staged by Augustus Caesar and
            Marcus Agrippa.

**AD**

14          Death of Augustus (reigns 27 BC–AD 14, first
            emperor of Rome. Succeeded by Tiberius.

64          Great Fire of Rome (18–19 July), used by Nero
            to initiate persecution of Rome's Christians.

68          Nero (reigns 54–68) dies by suicide, provoking
            civil war over the succession and the Year of
            the Four Emperors (69), from which Vespasian
            (reigns 69–79) and the Flavian Dynasty emerge
            victorious.

72–80       Construction of the Colosseum.

79–81　　　Reign of Titus.

80　　　　　Major fire in the Campus Martius, extending to the Capitoline hill. Its destruction
presages a major building campaign under
Domitian, including the Stadium of Domitian
(present-day Piazza Navona) and the Pantheon
(destroyed 110).

81–96　　　Reign of Domitian. Following his assassination,
Nerva succeeds him to the throne.

98–117　　Reign of Trajan. Consecration of the Forum of
Trajan in 113.

113　　　　Trajan invades Parthian Empire. His successor,
Hadrian, withdraws in 118.

117–38　　Reign of Hadrian. Reconstruction of the
Pantheon initiated in 118, in the same year as
work commenced on Hadrian's Villa at Tivoli.
Hadrian's Wall begun in 122, marking the
British edge of the Roman Empire.

132–6　　Bar Kokhba revolt against Rome (Third Jewish–
Roman War). Rome aggressively suppresses
Judean uprising.

191　　　　Fire rages in the area around the Forum, dam-
aging the imperial palace and the Temple of
Peace.

193　　　　Year of Five Emperors and civil war, precipitated
by the death of Commodus (reigns 180–92).
Commencement of the Severan dynasty of six
emperors (193–235).

212　　　　All free individuals living in the Roman Empire
granted citizenship.

| | |
|---|---|
| 217 | Fire damages the Colosseum, with reconstruction spanning to 240. |
| 235 | Assassination of Severus Alexander, provoking the Crisis of the Third Century. |
| 260–74 | Roman Empire split into three states: the Gallic Empire (under Postumus), the Palmyrene Empire (under Zenobia and Vabalathus) and the Roman Empire in Italy, between them. Reunited under Aurelian. |
| 272–9 | A new city wall – the Aurelian Wall – constructed under Aurelian and Probus. |
| 286 | Capital of the Western Roman Empire moved (by Diocletian) from Rome to Milan, or Mediolanum. |
| 286–305 | Maximian reigns as Augustus of the West. |
| 293 | Diocletian (reigns 284–305) divides the Roman Empire into Western and Eastern Empires, and establishes rule by Tetrarchy. Diocletian thereafter Augustus of the East. |
| 309–12 | Aurelian Wall raised in height under Maxentius. |
| 312 | Battle of the Milvian Bridge (Saxa Rubra, 28 October). |
| 313 | Edict of Milan (legalizing Christianity). |
| 324 | Constantine's imperium extends to the Eastern Roman Empire, once more unifying the Roman Empire under a single ruler. |
| 319/22–9 | Construction of the (Old) Basilica of St Peter. |
| 330 | Foundation of Constantinople as seat of the Eastern Roman Empire. |

| | |
|---|---|
| 346 | Public pagan worship within Rome prohibited by imperial decree. |
| 367 | City prefect restores the porticus deorum consentium, honouring twelve of Rome's gods. |
| 394 | Temple of Vesta restored. |
| 400(?) | Temple of Saturn restored in an early imperial style. |
| 402–3 | Honorius strengthens the Aurelian Wall in anticipation of Gothic siege. Imperial capital moved from Milan to Ravenna. |
| 408 | Theodosius II (Eastern Emperor, 408–50) decrees that Roman temples be repurposed to secular ends. |
| 410 | Sack of Rome by the Visigoth king Alaric I. Roman Army withdraws from Britain. |
| 435 | Final games staged at the Colosseum. |
| 455 | Sack of Rome by Vandals under King Gaiseric. |
| 455–76 | Chaos ensues. Rule of nine emperors between 455 and 476. |
| 459 | Legalization of spoliation (repurposing of building materials) where a building or monument is deemed to be beyond repair. |
| 476 | Deposition of Romulus Augustulus by Odoacer and the end of the Western Roman Empire. |
| 480 | Zeno dissolves the division of the Roman Empire into Western and Eastern Empires. Reclaims sole rule over a united (but diminished) Roman Empire. Rome subject to Constantinople until 800. |
| 520s | Last animal hunts staged at the Colosseum. |

527–65     Reign of Emperor Justinian, who seeks to restore the Roman Empire to its full extent.

536     Belisarius briefly captures Rome from the Ostrogoth Kingdom.

552     Rome recaptured for the Eastern Roman Empire by Justinian's forces, expelling the northern occupiers – his third effort to restore the city since 536. The Gothic War between the Ostrogoth Kingdom (occupying Rome) and the Eastern Roman Empire spanned 535–54.

568     Longobard (Lombard) invasion of Italy. Rome remains part of the Byzantine Empire but surrounded by Longobard lands.

578     Longobard siege of Rome – unsuccessfully concludes in 579, but results in a papal election without the blessing of the Byzantine emperor Tiberius Constantine.

590     Election of Gregory (the Great; St Gregory, reigns to 604); his reign held to have overseen the transition within the Church from Roman Christianity to the reassertion of Christianity as a European religion.

593     Lombard duke Ariulf invades Roman lands, but is dissuaded by Gregory from invading Rome. Returns 593/4 and peace is once more bought by ransom.

609     The Pantheon consecrated as a Christian church, this being the first sacralization of a pagan temple.

| | |
|---|---|
| 625–38 | Conversion by Honorius of the Senate House on the Forum Romanum into the Church of Sant'Adriano. |
| 640 | Muslim occupation of Jerusalem, rendering Rome the principal Holy City of Christendom. |
| 640 | First guides written for pilgrims to Rome. |
| 663/7 | Emperor Constans II visits Rome, during the pontificate of Vitalian (657–72), being the last Byzantine emperor to do so. |
| 711 | Emperor Justinian II and Pope Constantine unsuccessfully meet in Constantinople to resolve tensions between imperial rule and ecclesiastical authority. |
| 716 | One of four floods of the Tiber mentioned in the *Liber Pontificalis*, the others being 791, 856 and 860. |
| 731 | Gregory III is elected by acclamation, without imperial confirmation. |
| 753 | Rome besieged by Lombards, with peace negotiated by Pope Stephen II. |
| 772 | King Desiderius of Lombardy enters Rome, but is conquered by Charlemagne, who in 774 becomes King of the Lombards. |
| 795–816 | Pontificate of Leo III, which foments an ideological and political break with Constantinople. |
| 800 | Christmas Day: coronation of Charlemagne as Holy Roman Emperor. |
| 817–24 | Zeno Chapel built at Santa Prassede. |
| 823 | Pope Paschal I crowns Lothair as King of Italy, establishing precedent for the papal privilege of coronation in Rome. |

| | |
|---|---|
| 824 | Lothair asserts imperial authority over Rome, issuing a constitution in favour of Pope Gregory IV but asserting the need for imperial confirmation over civic matters and papal elections. |
| 843 | Rome and the Lands of St Peter (Papal States) named a fiefdom of the Roman Emperor (King of the Franks). |
| 846 | Sack of Rome by Saracens, presaging the construction of the wall around the Leonine City (Leonine Wall, constructed 846–53). |
| 872 | Sacralization of the temple of Fortuna Virilis (sometime during 872–82) as the second ancient temple repurposed for Christian worship. |
| 915–24 | Imperial reign of Berengar of Friuli (King of Italy 887–915), crowned emperor by John X to secure support against Saracen invasion from the south. |
| 962 | Otto I (the Great) crowned Holy Roman Emperor by John XII (reigns until 1002). Otto seeks to depose John in 964. |
| 966 | Otto puts down a civic uprising led by the city prefect Pietro. |
| 971–81 | Emperor Otto II restores Benedict VII to the papacy following the antipapacy of Boniface VII, seized after the death of Benedict VI. |
| 996–1002 | Reign of Otto III, in which he begins building an imperial palace in Rome. |
| 1059 | Creation of the College of Cardinals, part of the Investiture Controversy spanning from the 1050s to the Concordat of Worms. |

| | |
|---|---|
| 1075 | Gregory VII asserts that the pope alone may depose an emperor. Kidnapped and imprisoned at Christmas Mass in Santa Maria Maggiore. He then excommunicates and deposes Henry IV in 1076. |
| 1080 | Emperor Henry IV lays siege to Rome, occupying the Leonine City in 1083. |
| 1084 | Norman Sack of Rome under Robert Guiscard, prompted by military action to free Gregory VII from siege by Emperor Henry IV. |
| 1111 | Henry V invades Rome to be crowned emperor by Pope Paschal II. |
| 1117 | Henry V returns, forcing Paschal into exile. |
| 1122 | Concordat of Worms between Pope Callixtus II and Emperor Henry V, ending disputes over investiture. |
| 1130 | Double papal election following the death of Honorius II, with Innocent II and Anacletus II competing for legitimacy and temporal rule until the death of Anacletus in 1138. |
| 1143/4 | Establishment of the Commune of Rome. |
| 1150 | Senate palace for the Commune built on the Capitoline hill (first meeting held in 1151). |
| 1155 | Frederick Barbarossa turns down coronation by the Senate, but is crowned in St Peter's by Adrian IV. |
| 1188 | Papal recognition of the Commune of Rome. Peace negotiated by Clement III. |
| 1198–1216 | Papal reign of Innocent III, who convenes the Fourth Lateran Council in 1215. |

| | |
|---|---|
| 1208 | Construction of a fortified papal residence on the Vatican, the basis of the Apostolic Palace, under the authority of Innocent III. |
| 1215 | Fourth Lateran Council, which proclaims papal primacy. |
| 1231 | Flooding destroys the second-century (rebuilt) Pons Aemilius, now surviving in a ruined state as the Ponte Rotto. |
| 1257 | Works recorded on a new Palazzo Senatorio on the Capitoline hill. |
| 1277 | Relocation by Nicholas III of the seat of the papacy from the Lateran Palace, alongside the Cathedral of Rome, to the Vatican, alongside (Old) St Peter's Basilica. |
| 1300 | First Jubilee Year declared by Pope Boniface VIII, invoking the tradition of the Secular Games. |
| 1302 | Boniface VIII issues the bull *Unam sanctam* (directed at Philip IV of France), asserting the subordination of temporal rulers to the pontiff. Philip is excommunicated (1303) and French forces collaborate with the Colonna family to depose the pope (who dies before the year is out). |
| 1308 | Basilica of St John Lateran seriously damaged by fire. |
| 1309 | Clement V moves the Curia to Avignon. |
| 1347 | Revolt and tribuneship of Cola di Rienzo (May–December). |
| 1361 | Basilica of St John Lateran once again badly damaged by fire. |

1377      Gregory XI returns the Curia to Rome, thus ending the Avignon papacy.

1378–1417  Western Schism, marked by two papal lines of succession (Rome and Avignon).

1390      Jubilee Year named by Urban VI to (prematurely) celebrate the restitution of the papacy to Rome.

1417      Martin V elected to the papacy (1417–31), which is returned to Rome in 1420. The election occurs at the Council of Constance (1414–18).

1423      Jubilee Year named by Martin V to mark the end of the Western Schism, the return of stability to Church governance and (again) the return of the Curia to Rome.

1447      Election of Pope Nicholas V (Parentucelli), who reigns until 1454.

1450      Jubilee Year declared by Nicholas V, in which the Curia emerges as the city's governing body, with a major expansion of responsibilities for the civic management of amenities and building programmes.

1452      Coronation by Nicholas V of Frederick III as Holy Roman Emperor, being the last such coronation held in Rome.

1453      Restoration of the *mostra* of what would become the Fontana di Trevi. Siege and capitulation of Constantinople to the Ottoman Empire, under Sultan Mehmed II. Republican uprising against Nicholas V led by self-styled

Tribune Stefano Porcari (Stefano the Proud), who is duly executed.

1471–84    Papacy of Sixtus IV (della Rovere), whose achievements include the construction of the Vatican Library (1471–5) and the Sistine Chapel in the Apostolic Palace (1473–83).

1492–1503  Papacy of Alexander VI (Borgia).

1506       Foundation stone laid for the New Basilica of St Peter.

1508–12    Ceiling of the Sistine Chapel is painted by Michelangelo – a commission by Pope Julius II (della Rovere, reigns 1503–13).

1517       Martin Luther affixes his ninety-five theses to the door of the castle church in Wittenberg – one of the provocations leading to the Protestant Reformation.

1527–8     Sack of Rome by the troops of Holy Roman Emperor Charles V.

1534       Charles V processes through Rome and takes communion from Paul III, bringing an end to the hostilities and advancing reparations from the Sack of 1527.

1538       King Henry VIII of England excommunicated by Pope Paul III (Farnese), who reigns 1534–49.

1540       Foundation of the Society of Jesus under (St) Ignatius of Loyola.

1563       Conclusion of the Council of Trent (held 1545–63).

1575       Formation of the Congregation of the Oratory of St Philip Neri. Its mother church

|          | is built to the design of Francesco Borromini, 1637–50. |
|----------|---------|
| 1585–90  | Papacy of Sixtus V, marked by an intense public building programme, including churches, aqueducts, erection of obelisks, new arterial streets and the restoration of many significant buildings that had fallen into disrepair. |
| 1600     | Execution of Giordano Bruno (commemorated in a statue in the Campo dei Fiori). |
| 1618–48  | Thirty Years War. |
| 1623–44  | Papacy of Urban VIII (Barberini), who summons Galileo Galilei to Rome to recant his scientific work. |
| 1644–55  | Papacy of Innocent X (Pamphili), in which he develops the area of Piazza Navona by commissioning fountains by Bernini and a new façade for Sant'Agnese by Borromini. |
| 1655–67  | Reign of Alexander VII (Chigi), which witnesses the construction of major new churches, streets and public squares. |
| 1666     | Founding of the French Academy in Rome. |
| 1702     | Accademia di San Luca commences staging student *concorsi* (competitions) for public buildings, monuments and piazzas. |
| 1725     | Spanish Steps completed to the design of Francesco de Sanctis. |
| 1732–72  | Design and construction of the Trevi Fountain. |
| 1738–48  | Survey and preparation of the *Pianta grande di Roma* by Giambattista Nolli, commissioned by Benedict XIV. |

| 1754–65 | Roman sojourn of the French painter Hubert Robert (1733–1808). |
|---|---|
| 1776–89 | Publication by Edward Gibbon of *The History of the Decline and Fall of the Roman Empire*. |
| 1798–9 | Napoleonic Roman Republic, which forces Pope Pius VI into exile. |
| 1809 | Pius VII in exile following the French annexation of the Papal States. |
| 1846 | Election of Pius IX (reigns 1846–78). |
| 1848 | Pius IX escapes Rome in the face of a democratic uprising. |
| 1849 | Roman Republic declared 9 February (invoking Mazzini's notion of a Third Rome). Papal rule restored with French support, 3 July. |
| 1861 | Kingdom of Italy founded. |
| 1870 | Defeat of papal forces by Garibaldi's Italian troops and entry through the Porta Pia, resulting in the dissolution of the Papal States in 1871. |
| 1871 | Rome becomes the third capital of the Kingdom of Italy after Turin (1861–5) and Florence (1865–71). |
| 1873 | Rome adopts its first regulatory plan, anticipating substantial population growth. |
| 1883 | Rome adopts a revised regulatory plan predicating the city's spread into large parts of hitherto undeveloped land. |
| 1909 | City of Rome adopts a new regulatory plan that anticipates development beyond the Aurelian Wall. |

| | |
|---|---|
| 1922 | Benito Mussolini (1883–1945) elected as Italy's twenty-seventh Prime Minister (1922–43) – 'Duce' of the Italian Fascist Party, 1919–45. |
| 1929 | Lateran Treaty and establishment of the Vatican City. |
| 1936 | Italy expelled from the League of Nations after invading Ethiopia. |
| 1943–4 | German occupation of Rome following Italy's surrender to Allied Forces (1943) and realignment as a cobelligerent against Germany. Vatican bombed (1943–4). |
| 1948 | Establishment of the Republic of Italy with Rome as its capital. |
| 1957 | Treaty of Rome signed, under which Italy joined the European Economic Community (later European Union). |
| 1960 | Rome hosts the Games of the XVII Olympiad. |
| 1968 | 'Battle of Valle Giulia' between leftist militants and police in the area around the Facoltà di Architettura and the British School at Rome. A key episode in the protests of *sessantotto* (1968). |
| 1978 | Assassination of Christian Democratic President Aldo Moro by members of the Red Brigades. |
| 1993–2001 | Mayoralty of Francesco Rutelli. |
| 1994 | Silvio Berlusconi first elected Prime Minister of the Republic of Italy (serving 1994–5, 2001–6, 2008–11). |
| 2005 | Death of Pope John Paul II (Wojtyła, reigns 1978–2005). |

2007        Beginning of the Global Financial Crisis. City-wide protests against economic conditions held 15 October 2011.

2013        Resignation of Pope Benedict XVI, followed by the election of Pope Francis.

2015        Resignation of Ignazio Marino as Mayor of Rome (mayoralty 2013–15).

# Notes

**Preface**

1 Jesse Benedict Carter, 'The Evolution of the City of Rome from its Origin to the Gallic Catastrophe', *Proceedings of the American Philosophical Society* 48, no. 192 (1909), 129.

**Introduction: Thinking about Seeing**

1 Georg Simmel, 'Rome' (1898), trans. Ulrich Teucher and Thomas M. Kemple, *Theory, Culture & Society* 24, nos 7–8 (2007), 31.

2 Simmel, 'Rome', 35.

3 Simmel, 'Rome', 32–3.

4 Simmel, 'Rome', 34.

5 Sigmund Freud, *The Interpretation of Dreams*, trans. James Strachey (London: Allen & Unwin, 1955), 194.

6 Freud, *Civilization and Its Discontents*, trans. Joan Riviere (London: The Hogarth Press and the Institute of Psychoanalysis, 1973), 7–8.

7 Freud, *Civilization and Its Discontents*, 8.

8 Georg Simmel, 'Venice' (1907), trans. Ulrich Teucher and Thomas M. Kemple, *Theory, Culture & Society* 24, nos 7–8 (2007), 44.

9 Mary Beard, 'Why Ancient Rome Matters to the Modern World', *Guardian* (2 October 2015), online at http://www.theguardian.com/books/2015/oct/02/mary-beard-why-ancient-rome-matters. The article previews *SPQR: A History of Ancient Rome* (London: Profile, 2015).

10 Lauro de Bosis, 'Histoire de ma mort', *Le Soir*, 3 October 1931; *The Story of My Death*, ed. Ruth Draper (Oxford: Oxford University Press, 1933), anthologized in *Fascism, Anti-fascism, and the Resistance in Italy, 1919 to the Present*, ed. Stanislaus G. Pugliese (Oxford: Rowman & Littlefield, 2004), 115–19, quoting from 118, with slight rearrangement of the translation. His ammunition was an Italian translation of Bolton King's newly published *Fascism in Italy* (London: Williams & Norgate, 1931).

**Chapter 1  A Matter of Foundations**

1   Virgil, *The Aeneid* (19 BC), I, trans. John Dryden, online at http://classics.mit.edu/Virgil/aeneid.html.

2   T. P. Wiseman, *Remus: A Roman Myth* (Cambridge: Cambridge University Press, 1995), xiv; see also 54–5, 62, 76. J. E. Lendon defends the Roman historians in 'Historians without History: Against Roman Historians', in *The Cambridge Companion to the Roman Historians*, ed. Andrew Feldherr (Cambridge: Cambridge University Press, 2009), 41–61.

3   Pierre Grimal, *Civilization of Ancient Rome*, trans. W. S. Maguinness (London: George Allen & Unwin, 1963), 39.

4   This follows Christopher Smith, 'The Beginnings of Urbanization in Rome', in *Mediterranean Urbanization 800–600 BC*, ed. Robin Osborne and Barry Cunliffe (Oxford: Oxford University Press, 2005), 104–5; and Wiseman, *Remus*, 156.

5   Christopher Smith, *Early Rome and Latium: Economy and Society c.1000 to 500 BC* (Oxford: Clarendon Press, 1996), 5.

6   Andrea Carandini, *Rome: Day One*, trans. Stephen Sartarelli (Princeton, NJ: Princeton University Press, 2011), 15.

7   These paragraphs summarize the much more fine-grained analysis of sites, materials and construction techniques by Seth G. Bernard in 'Continuing the Debate on Rome's Earliest Circuit Walls', *Papers of the British School at Rome* 80 (2012), 13–35.

8   David Watkin, *The Roman Forum* (London: Profile, 2009).

9   Amanda Claridge, *Rome: An Oxford Archaeological Guide* (Oxford: Oxford University Press, 1998; 2nd edn, 2010); Touring Club Italiano, *Guida d'Italia: Roma* (1925; Milan: Touring Club Italiano, 10th edn, 2008).

10   Walter Dennison, 'The Roman Forum as Cicero Saw It', *Classical Journal* 3, no. 8 (1908), 320.

11   Dennison, 'The Roman Forum as Cicero Saw It', 319.

12   Dennison, 'The Roman Forum as Cicero Saw It', 325.

13   Polybius, *The Histories*, Book I, online at http://penelope.uchicago.edu/Thayer/E/Roman/Texts/Polybius/1*.html.

14   Tacitus, *The Annals*, Book I, online at http://classics.mit.edu/Tacitus/annals.1.i.html.

## Chapter 2 *Roma Caput Mundi*

1 Much of this summary draws from Amanda Claridge, *Rome: An Oxford Archaeological Guide*, 2nd edn (Oxford: Oxford University Press, 2010), 312–19.

2 William Smith, William Wayte and G. E. Marindin, 'Ludi', in *A Dictionary of Greek and Roman Antiquities* (London: John Murray, 1890), online at http://www.perseus.tufts.edu/hopper/collections/.

3 Samuel Johnson, reviewing *Memoires of the Court of Augustus* by Thomas Blackwell, *Literary Magazine* 1 (1756), 41.

4 Quoted in Claridge, *Rome*, 306.

5 Indra Kagis McEwen, 'Hadrian's Rhetoric I: The Pantheon', *RES: Anthropology and Aesthetics* 24 (1993), 57.

6 Adam Ziolkowski, 'Was Agrippa's Pantheon the Temple of Mars "in Campo"?' *Papers of the British School at Rome* 62 (1994), 261–77.

7 McEwen, 'Hadrian's Rhetoric I', 59–63.

8 Quoted in Tod A. Marder, 'Alexander VII, Bernini, and the Urban Setting of the Pantheon in the Seventeenth Century', *Journal of the Society of Architectural Historians* 50, no. 3 (1991), 276.

## Chapter 3 A Middle Age

1 Ramsay MacMullen, *Constantine* (London: Weidenfeld & Nicolson, 1970), 110, paraphrased in Richard Krautheimer, *Three Christian Capitals: Topography and Politics* (Berkeley: University of California Press, 1983), 35.

2 Krautheimer, *Three Christian Capitals*, 26, 28–30, 36–8.

3 Richard Krautheimer, *Rome: Profile of a City, 312–1309* (Princeton, NJ: Princeton University Press, 1980), 61.

4 Krautheimer, *Rome*, 62.

5 R. H. C. Davis, *A History of Medieval Europe from Constantine to Saint Louis*, 2nd edn (London: Longman, 1988), 139–40.

6 Cited in Éamonn Ó Carragain and Carol Neuman de Vegvar (eds), *Roma Felix: Formations and Reflections of Medieval Rome* (Farnham: Ashgate, 2007), 1.

7 Alan Thacker, 'Rome of the Martyrs: Saints, Cults and Relics, Fourth to Seventh Centuries', in *Roma Felix*, eds Ó Carragain and Neuman de Vegvar, 13–49; also Debra J. Birch, *Pilgrimage to Rome in the Middle Ages: Continuity and Change* (Woodbridge: Boydell Press, 1998), 92–3.

8   Caroline J. Goodson, 'Archaeology and the Cult of Saints in the Early Middle Ages: Accessing the Sacred', *Mélanges de L'École française de Rome – Moyen Âge* 126, no. 1 (2014), online at http://mefrm.revues.org/1818.

9   Krautheimer offers a catalogue of the ancient monuments known to twelfth-century Romans in *Rome*, 187–8.

10  See Louis I. Hamilton, 'Memory, Symbol, and Arson: Was Rome "Sacked" in 1084?', *Speculum* 78, no. 2 (2003), 378–99.

11  Krautheimer, *Rome*, 150–1.

12  Krautheimer, *Rome*, 152–3.

13  James Ackerman, *The Architecture of Michelangelo* (1961; London: Pelican, 1970), 145–63.

### Chapter 4  Return to Rome

1   Manfredo Tafuri, *Interpreting the Renaissance: Princes, Cities, Architecture*, trans. Daniel Sherer (1992; New Haven, Conn.: Yale University Press, 2006), 35–6.

2   Cited by Tafuri, *Interpreting the Renaissance*, 35.

3   Tafuri, *Interpreting the Renaissance*, 36–7.

4   Maarten Delbeke, *The Art of Religion: Sforza Pallavicino and Art Theory in Bernini's Rome* (Farnham: Ashgate, 2012), 98–103.

5   Leon Battista Alberti, *On the Art of Building in Ten Books*, trans. Joseph Rykwert, Neil Leach and Robert Tavenor (Cambridge, Mass.: MIT Press, 1988), 362.

6   Valeria Cafà, 'The via Papalis in Early Cinquecento Rome: A Contested Space between Roman Families and Curials', *Urban History* 37, no. 3 (2010), 435. See also Nicholas Temple, *Renovatio Urbis: Architecture, Urbanism and Ceremony in the Rome of Julius II* (London: Routledge, 2011), 27, 56–7.

7   Tafuri in Luigi Salerno, Luigi Spezzaferro and Manfredo Tafuri, *Via Giulia. Una utopia urbanistica del 500* (Rome: Aristide Staderini, 1973), 152.

8   Lex Bosman, *The Power of Tradition: Spolia in the Architecture of St Peter's in the Vatican* (Hilversum: Uitgeverij Verloren, 2004), 136–8.

9   Bosman, *The Power of Tradition*, 135–6.

10  André Chastel, *The Sack of Rome, 1527*, trans. Beth Archer (Princeton, NJ: Princeton University Press, 1983), 4.

11  Chastel, *The Sack of Rome*, 91.

12  Quoted in Chastel, *The Sack of Rome*, 106.

13  Chastel, *The Sack of Rome*, 214.

14  Nicholas V cited by Tafuri, *Interpreting the Renaissance*, 29.

15  Thomas De Quincey, *Confessions of an English Opium-Eater* (1821; London: Wordsworth Classics, 1994), 188–9.

**Chapter 5  The Capital of Italy**

 1  Spiro Kostof, 'The Drafting of a Master Plan for *Roma Capitale*: An Exordium', *Journal of the Society of Architectural Historians* 35, no. 1 (March 1976), 5.

 2  Spiro Kostof, 'The Third Rome: The Polemics of Architectural History', *Journal of the Society of Architectural Historians* 32, no. 3 (1973), 240.

 3  Paul Ginsborg, *A History of Contemporary Italy, 1943–1980* (London: Penguin, 1990), 247.

 4  Terry Kirk, *The Architecture of Modern Italy*, Vol. 2 (New York: Princeton Architectural Press, 2005), 148.

 5  Manfredo Tafuri, 'Bianchi, Salvatore', *Dizionario biografico degli Italiani*, Vol. 10 (Rome: Istituto della Enciclopedia italiana, 1968), 174.

 6  Kirk, *The Architecture of Modern Italy*, Vol. 2, 105–7, 153–5.

 7  Stephanie Pilat, *Reconstructing Italy: The Ina-Casa Neighborhoods of the Post-War Era* (Farnham: Ashgate, 2014), 237, 184–94.

# Credits

*Figure sources*: 0.1: Huey Jean Tan; 0.2: Alexandra Brown; 0.3: *Opere di Giovanni Battista Piranesi, Francesco Piranesi e d'altri*, Vol. 10 (Paris: Firmin Didot Freres, 1835–9), Wikimedia Commons; 1.1: Manfred Heyde, Wikimedia Commons; 1.2: Rabax63, Wikimedia Commons; 1.3: Wikimedia Commons; 1.4: Jean-Pierre Dalbéra, Wikimedia Commons; 1.5: Originally published in the *Classical Journal* 3, no. 8 (1908); 2.1 and 2.2: Jean-Pierre Dalbéra, Wikimedia Commons; 2.3: Romualdo Moscioni, Wikimedia Commons; 2.4: Samuel H. Kress Collection, National Gallery of Art, Washington, DC, image in public domain; 3.1: Andrew Leach; 3.2: Map by Giacomo Lauro and Antonio Tempestra showing the Seven Pilgrim Churches of Rome, c. 1600. Wikimedia Commons; 3.3: Valerio B. Cosentino, Wikimedia Commons; 3.4: Metropolitan Museum of Art, New York (www.metmuseum.org); 4.1: Andrew Leach; 4.2: British Museum, London © Trustees of the British Museum; 4.3: Marie-Lan Nguyen, Wikimedia Commons; 4.4, 4.5, and 5.1: Wikimedia Commons; 5.2: Cartella XIII, 119: Piante e immagini di Roma e del Lazio (Archivio Storico Capitolino), Rome; 5.3: Fotocollectie Algemeen Nederlands Fotopersbureau,

Nationaal Archief, Den Haag; 5.4: Jean-Pierre Dalbéra. Wikimedia Commons.

# Index of Works

# Index of Places

# Index of Names